The Accountability Edge

The Accountability Edge

By
Debbie O'Grady

Copyright © 2014 by Hunter's Moon Publishing
ISBN Paperback: 978-1-937988-14-2
ISBN Kindle: 978-1-937988-15-9

Hunter's Moon Publishing
http://HuntersMoonPublishing.com

Dedication

This book is dedicated to the people who helped shape me into the person I am today. They may not have always understood what it is I am doing but they have always supported me.

My Mom and Dad were the first people to tell me I could do anything I wanted with my life and they showed by example how true that was. My wonderful sister Muriel is always there for me with words of encouragement and my brother Billy (I'm the only one he lets get away with still calling him that) is the strongest person I know - body, mind and spirit. These are four people I've looked up to and admired all my life.

I also dedicate this book to my husband, John. He has been my rock from the very beginning of this entrepreneurial journey I have undertaken and I love him dearly for being brave enough to let me experiment and find my own way in my own time.

Table of Contents

Introduction

Whenever I hear or read about a person or company that became an overnight success, I always read further to find out how long it actually took to become that "overnight success." I know it's not reality that someone opens their business on a Monday and is making a 6 or 7 figure income by Friday (or even a month from Friday) – my definition of "overnight success."

When I find out it took two to three years, I'm still very impressed (actually anything less than five years is impressive to me) and I want to know what exactly was done to gain that success. The questions I want answers to are ones like – How did they know to do what they did? Who helped them along the way? Where did they find the information that helped them to succeed?

I know they didn't become successful by doing things alone. More than likely, they each had a lot of help along the way, through training, coaching, and mentoring. I want to hear about those experiences and the lessons they learned on their journey to success. The itch for these answers compelled me to select fifteen successful entrepreneurs and ask them to share their experiences, insights, and tips. That is the information I want to share with you, in this book.

As I asked questions of each of these entrepreneurs about how they got where they currently are in their business, I heard more and more tell me about the "edge" accountability had given them in accomplishing their goals and attaining their successes. The *Accountability Edge* story each shared was a little bit different and unique for each individual. Each chapter of this book contains the experiences and lessons learned from one of the fifteen entrepreneurs, plus me, centered on the topic of Accountability. You'll see, as you read, that each chapter author has a different view of the meaning of accountability as they tell how that *Accountability Edge* helped them in their success.

I invite you to dive right in with Chapter One, written by Michele Scism, where she shares inspirational stories of how accountability has helped her clients – and also how it has helped her –succeed, often beyond her own expectations.

Connie Ragen Green shares her first experiences with goal setting and accountability in Chapter Two. Even at a young age, Connie saw the benefits of having an accountability partner to help her attain her goals.

Nicole Dean's examples of how accountability has worked for both her business and her clients may be just the motivation that helps move you to create your own "challenges". Read this in Chapter Three.

In Chapter Four, Kathleen Gage recounts a 24-hour period when she was first praised by one audience for the message she shared and then booed and told to "get off the stage" by the next audience, who had been given the exact same talk. Kathleen's story communicates the ups and downs almost everyone has faced, and her personal insights are an inspiration and roadmap for getting past the roadblocks to get to where you can celebrate your successes.

You can read about Paul Taubman's experiences with accountability in Chapter Five, and his take on responsibility and having fun with it.

Birgitta Jorgenson shares her experiences of using an Accountability Coach to help her accomplish some big goals in Chapter Six. She also offers Three Tips to guide you to accomplish your goals.

In Chapter Seven, you can read how Adrienne Dupree puts that sometimes "nasty" word – accountability – into a good light and uses it to her benefit.

Kathi Laughman identifies what she believes are the five essential keys to make accountability work for you to achieve your goals. You can read this from Kathi in Chapter Eight.

Geoff Hoff lays out his experiences with accountability partners; what has worked and what has not, in Chapter Nine. He offers Six Main Questions you should ask yourself when deciding on an accountability relationship.

Chapter Ten is written by Faydra Koenig who offers examples for hope, from her own experiences, to others who may feel helpless and hopeless in a situation they didn't create.

Felicia Slattery's recommendations, in Chapter Eleven, about what to look for and how to manage an accountability partnership, are based on years of experience with many different accountability partners.

Meredith Eisenberg shares Seven Tips and Other Insights on how to create accountability in your business to control technology and succeed. She writes about this in Chapter Twelve.

Read lucky Chapter Thirteen for Adam Urbanski's insightful advice about using both internal and external accountability, and why he feels cheerleaders are so important to your business.

In Chapter Fourteen, Kristen Eckstein states "if you are not accountable to anyone except yourself, I urge you to change that as soon as possible." She explains how you can find the people that will help you stay accountable and the reasons why you'll want to do that.

Leslie Cardinal gives ideas you can use to accelerate your goal achievement and create a great accountability structure in Chapter Fifteen

The final Chapter of this book is my own account of how I've used and taught accountability through the years to help people attain their goals.

My suggestion is to read this book from beginning to end rather than skip among the different chapters. You'll want to highlight and mark the pages you find most useful for yourself. As a special bonus, I've pulled out the lists of tips and questions from the different chapters and created a short report of all of them. You can download that list at: http://TheAccountabilityEdgeBook.com/Tips

Happy Reading and Always Keep Smiling!
Debbie

Chapter One

How an Accountability Call Made me $300,000 By Michele Scism

"You are the first person to let yourself off the hook if you don't get something done. You buy into your own stories. You are probably the best procrastinator you know."

Once upon a time there was a young woman who was living a double life. To her friends, family and the outside world, it looked like she had it all together. She was building a business, had written her first two books, had hosted her first three day event, and was traveling the world for speaking engagements. It looked as if she was on top of her game but her reality was a bit different. Yes, she was building a business but it wasn't profitable. Yes, she had written her first two books and hosted her first three day event but the books weren't selling and the event did not fill her coaching program like she was sure it would. Yes, she was traveling the world to speak but she wasn't making enough money from those speaking engagements to cover her expenses. The reality was that her business was hemorrhaging money and she was depleting her retirement account and maxing out her credit cards to keep things going.

Sounds painful, doesn't it? The sad reality is that it is the story that most entrepreneurs live until they either give up on their dreams or they make some drastic changes in the way they do business.

You might have guessed by now that this is not just the story of any entrepreneur, it is my story. I am Michele Scism, The 6-Figure Results Lady from DecisiveMinds.com. I am a business coach, author, international speaker, event host and radio show host. I work with entrepreneurs who are tired of living a double life and are seriously ready to make money. In a little bit, I will tell you the rest of my story and you will see that it doesn't have to be this way. The good news is that I was able to turn my business into a profitable, thriving enterprise.

How to go From Struggling Entrepreneur to Profitable Entrepreneur!

As a business coach I know that struggling entrepreneurs usually have problems with three areas:

- Figuring out a marketing message that will attract their ideal client.
- Designing products, programs and services that their clients are looking for.
- Knowing what to say to close the sale.

You have probably taken classes, listened to lots of teleseminars and learned tons of strategies to tweak your marketing message, sell more and make more money. So why haven't things changed in your business? The reason is because you haven't implemented what you have learned.

The reason you haven't implemented what you have learned is because **you** are in charge of **you**. You might have heard people say "I work for the best boss in the world – ME!" Well, I beg to differ. You are the first person to let yourself off the hook if you don't get something done. You buy into your own stories. You are probably the best procrastinator you know. I have worked with hundreds of entrepreneurs and I see it over and over. You make great plans, take off like a jolt and get side tracked and before you know it the day, the week, the month is gone and you are wondering why the program didn't fill or you didn't get any new clients.

It's a double edged sword. Most of us are entrepreneurs because we either don't want to work for someone else or we describe ourselves as non-employable. However, not having that person to hold us responsible is also a problem. What we need is accountability. We need someone to be accountable to.

Accountability comes in many forms. You meet some amazing people at an event and decide to hold each other accountable. You start out with great calls and people are really showing up and helping each other and then within weeks you notice people start to not show. This is usually because they aren't doing what they have said they would and they don't want to tell you. They don't really want to be held accountable. I know because I have participated in these types of groups. Some of them lasted a while but inevitably they all fail. I think another reason they don't make it is because no one has skin in the game. In other words, they are not paying to be held responsible. You have a different mindset when you are paying for it.

That brings me to the form of accountability that I think works – hiring someone to hold you accountable. It might be someone who specializes in accountability or a coach in the specific area you need to be held accountable in. For my own business, this is what made it turn around. I have always worked with a coach and the coaches that I've worked with were great at holding my feet to the fire. If I didn't do what I said I was going to do they called me on it. What I found was that for me, it worked because I liked them and didn't want to disappoint them. Whatever it takes – right! They helped me to get a grip on my spending, better understand my pricing and held me responsible for making the contacts and phone calls that it took to fill my programs and events. It was a total shift for me.

How to use Accountability in Your Business

After turning my business around and realizing that so many of my clients were having the same issues I started to look at ways to be more strategic when it came to accountability. Most entrepreneurs hire coaches because they are really looking for a partner, someone to tell them what to do and make sure they do it. However, for a lot of coaches that is not their strong point. They may be great with the strategy but they are lacking when it comes to holding their clients accountable for their commitments.

In 2013 I made the decision to make accountability a focus in my coaching programs. My clients work with me in one on one sessions every other week but in between those sessions they actually work with my accountability coach, Debbie O'Grady. Debbie keeps track of their commitments, what it is specifically they are working on and then checks to make sure they are taking the actions necessary to get everything done. We have seen a drastic increase in the productivity and growth of my clients businesses since putting this in place.

Jena is a great example. Jena is a branding coach and she saw the revenues in her coaching business almost triple in a 90 day period. She even had her first ever $30,000 month. I attribute this growth to the strategy that we created and the fact that the accountability calls kept her on track.

Joe and Jennifer are another great example. Joe is a motivational speaker and when we first started the process they were working on developing a new website, creating four new products, writing four new books and at the same time filling his speaking calendar. They completed the website, four products and four books in record time and finished out that year with record sales.

I told you I would share the rest of my story. So as I said earlier, since I started this coaching business, I have always had a business coach. I've done that for a couple of reasons. First, I want someone who has done what I want to do and can show me the short cuts, but maybe even bigger than that, I know that I work best when I have someone I have to answer to. Not a boss – this is different. This is someone who isn't going to buy into my story and will not take my excuses. Some coaches are better at this than others. So as you already know, that first year and a half was a real struggle but then things started to change. The company began to grow rapidly and in my fourth year in business I found myself at a crossroads.

I was hosting my own 3 day event where I was going to offer the audience an opportunity to coach with me. It was big. By far the biggest offer I had ever made. I was terrified because the event was costing me a lot of money and that little voice in my head was saying "Play it safe – go for a smaller offer so more of them can buy. Then you will definitely make enough money to cover the event." So the night before my offer I called my coach. I begged him to let me drop the price of my offer. He said "Absolutely not. And if you do drop the price don't call back." How's that for accountability? It was put up or shut up time. The following day I took a deep breath and took the stage to make my offer to the crowd. I could hear his voice saying "if you do drop the price don't call back." Long story and lots of shaking knees later, I finished that event with over $300,000 in revenues. That led to revenues that year of almost a half million dollars.

If he hadn't held me accountable I could have lost a lot of money. How many of you would have listened to that voice in your head because you don't have someone holding you responsible for your actions?

To be accountable simply means to be responsible to someone or to report, explain or justify what you are doing. Accountability has been a key part of my success and I know it would be for you. My advice is to find someone who is not your friend, who will not buy into your stories of why this won't work and who will not join in with your conversations of lack. You want someone who will be firm and call you out when you don't take the actions that are necessary to build a thriving business.

Michele Scism is a serial entrepreneur who knows how it feels to fail miserably at business - at one time the bank actually called demanding their $1.5 million back -but also knows how it *feels to sign the contract to sell your company for $9 million dollars. She's driven, she's decisive and she doesn't pull punches. Michele is a business coach, author, international speaker, radio show host and the founder of www.DecisiveMinds.com .*

Chapter Two

Accountability for Entrepreneurs
By Connie Ragen Green

"My friend Tory had done an excellent job of keeping me focused on what I had said I wanted and on track to see it through."

I'm an online marketing strategist and author, which means that I help others to build profitable businesses they can run from home, or from wherever in the world they happen to be. Being accountable is a huge part of success, so I was thrilled when I was asked to share my thoughts and experiences on this topic.

When I think about the concept of accountability and of being accountable, it also makes me think about taking responsibility and determining your own destiny. Perhaps this comes from my childhood, where I was surrounded by people who allowed other people and their situations to guide their daily actions. They became reactionary, rather than initiating their own goals and dreams. The result was that they were unhappy, bored with their lives, always complaining about not having enough money, and feeling like they were unlucky and the world was against them.

By the time I was twelve years old I had decided that my own life would not be like this if I could at all help it from becoming so. My mother and I had moved from Los Angeles to Miami, Florida and everything was new to me. This was right around the time I began earning my own money by babysitting, mowing lawns, and doing other odd jobs. The highest paying work I did during that summer was scraping barnacles off the sides and bottom of a boat. My knuckles were bloody and I was a sweaty mess, but I earned more over that weekend than I did during the entire remainder of the summer. By the time school started again in the fall I was able to purchase a new bicycle, all new clothes, start a savings account, and even give some money to my mother. I had taken responsibility and been accountable to myself to make this happen and I was very excited and proud of my results.

As we get older, life tends to get in the way of our dreams and goals, so by the time I was sixteen my motivation had dwindled and once again I found myself floundering. My successful summer four years earlier seemed like the distant past. Holding myself accountable just wasn't doing the trick, so I enlisted the help of two friends to help me get moving again that summer.

Kathy was a friend I had known since seventh grade. Even though she was very pretty and popular and I was very plain and more studious, our friendship had blossomed. She and I met at Arby's to have a roast beef sandwich and a milk shake and discussed what we wanted to accomplish during the next three months. This included losing ten pounds each, taking a trip together to Disney World, finding part-time jobs, and landing nice boyfriends to take us out to the movies and the beach.

Tory was a friend I had met just a year earlier, and we had hit it off right away. I shared my goals with him and he nodded in acknowledgement. I asked him what he wanted to do that summer and he thought for a moment before answering that he just wanted to have fun. I thought this was interesting, and no more was said about it.

Kathy and I drifted apart over the next couple of months, and when I did run into her at the shopping mall she admitted that she had gained five pounds since we last spoke, and that she had been fired from the job she got shortly after being hired. I gave her a hug and wished her well. I did find out later that she must have found a boyfriend, because her baby was born the following spring. She left school and no one ever heard from her again. I went to the apartment building where she had lived with her mother and younger siblings but they had moved and left no forwarding address.

My First Accountability Partner

By default, Tory had become my first accountability partner, even though we never used that term way back then.

During the first couple of weeks after we had originally discussed our goals, he had introduced me to a new neighbor who was now the manager of a local coffee shop and pancake house, and this man, Mr. Tucker, hired me to become a hostess three days a week. Tory had come in as a customer one day and somehow convinced one of the waitresses to let me take his order. This led to me asking for and being granted the opportunity to have three tables of my own every Sunday morning, where I raked in at least twenty dollars in tips.

He also introduced me to several of his friends, and one fellow and I really liked each other. His name was Nick, and that summer I officially had my first boyfriend. It was mostly platonic, but I enjoyed the attention and he was fun to be around. My mother approved and we saw each other most days to talk and spend time together. We saw *Escape From Planet of the Apes* and *The French Connection* at the movies, and made it to the beach at least once a week.

The week before school started Tory told Nick and I about a bus trip we could take up to the Orlando area so we could visit Disney World for the day. They were having their Grand Opening in a few weeks and wanted to give the local people an opportunity to visit while it was still brand new. The three of us left at four in the morning, and returned home just after midnight. It was a magical day that I will never forget, and on the bus ride home I remember thinking that everything I dreamed of for that summer had come true. Oh, and I had lost more than ten pounds, probably because I was so busy and having so much fun. My friend Tory had done an excellent job of keeping me focused on what I had said I wanted and on track to see it through.

My life went on, and I never gave another thought to what had occurred that summer of 1971 until many decades later. Tory and I remained friends until his untimely death in 2005, and I felt blessed to have had his friendship for so long. I always felt that he had done so much more for me than I had done for him, but his goal of wanting to have fun seemed to have been fulfilled on a regular basis throughout his life.

In my adult experience I became a classroom teacher and also worked in real estate. Once again I was surrounded by people who, for the most part, refused to take responsibility for their actions and chose to blame others when things did not work out as planned. For twenty years I struggled to maintain the motivation to excel in my work, and finally gave in to an existence of mediocrity. It was no wonder that in 2005, the year I would turn fifty years old, I would make the decision to leave that life behind and seek one where I could rise above my circumstances and change my life forever. No one was forcing me to do this, so I had to be completely accountable to myself if it was going to happen.

Was It Too Late For Me To Change My Life?

Making the transition from a salaried employee of the school district and a small business owner in the real estate business to that of an entrepreneur is not an easy one. All of a sudden you are in charge of making things happen in your life and in your business. You wake up in the morning, turn on your computer, and you're at work. There is no one calling you on the phone or knocking at your door to make sure you are on track to meet your goals. You might not even have any goals because you're not sure what to do. If you do nothing all day, you are the only one who knows that. Even your family cannot hold you accountable, for they do not even know what it is that you need to be doing. It's both exhilarating and frightening, and if you can do what needs to be done, the people around you will believe you are a superhero. At age fifty, with no previous experience in this world, I had thoughts that I might be too old to change and embrace this way of life. I desperately wanted my new life to be a joyous and successful one but wasn't sure how to make that happen.

After just a few months I became mired down in the tasks and activities that were required of me. I blogged out into cyberspace and hosted teleseminars with no one listening on the line. It felt as though I was spinning my wheels and could not gain any traction, even though I was working eight to ten hours each day. This was before social media, so it honestly felt like I was completely alone. This was when I decided to find a coach or a mentor to guide me through what I needed to do and to hold me accountable.

After some searching on the Internet I did find someone and paid him five thousand dollars up front for a year of coaching and accountability, but it was not a positive experience for me. He was busy with other students and just did not provide the level of help I was looking for. I take full responsibility for this, and decided right then to always hold myself accountable for my life and my business.

I honestly believe that when all is said and done you must be the one to make things happen for yourself. We cannot expect someone else to have the same passion and the commitment to our goals and dreams as we would. With that said, I do think it's valuable to be a part of a Mastermind group, especially one that meets in person a minimum of twice each year. That way people in the group can find someone else to work with as an accountability partner for a period of weeks or months, or for a special project. I run a group like this and my people receive great benefit from being a part of it.

Choosing The Right Accountability Model For You

The bottom line with this is that you must do what works for you. If you are doing an excellent job at holding yourself accountable, as I feel I do, then stick with that. If, on the other hand, you fail to accomplish your goals on a regular basis, or set goals that are too low then you may want to work with someone directly.

I still maintain that we must take full responsibility for our actions and circumstances, and that we can then determine our own destiny. If working with an accountability coach, such as Debbie O'Grady, makes sense for you, then know that you'll be working with someone whom I hold in the highest regard.

Entrepreneurs are wired differently than others, in that we receive our reward from doing things that have not been done before, or achieving goals that others told us could not be done. We are in our own little world much of the time. I do my best work early in the morning and find that I am able to tune out everything else until I accomplish what I set out to do. Accountability is the glue that holds us together, so find what is right for you and make it happen.

Connie Ragen Green is an online marketing strategist and bestselling author living in southern California. She teaches people on six continents how to build profitable online businesses so they may live the life they choose. Find out more at http://ConnieRagenGreen.com.

Chapter Three

"Challenge" Yourself To Accountability
By Nicole Dean

> *"Without accountability, it's too easy to just say "I'll get to that tomorrow" ... day after day after day and never ever end up reaching your goals."*

Hi and thanks for reading my chapter. I'm Nicole Dean, and I help Online Business owners to build profitable businesses that reach their financial and lifestyle goals – while making the web and the world a better place. In my mind, there's no point in creating a business that makes you miserable or that keeps you from spending time doing what you love. So, I find great joy in helping bloggers, authors, speakers, coaches and service providers to build in recurring revenue streams, ongoing profits, and solid cashflow by providing value to their audience and serving them well.

To me accountability means getting things done because of outside forces. We all have internal motivation for certain things, but not for the things we can easily put off. That's where external motivation can come in handy.

For instance, you may find it really easy to make your bed every morning. That doesn't require any accountability. But, you may be putting off publishing your book, because it's just "not ready yet". That may need a little outside help.

For me, personally, I find that I'll let myself down a hundred times a day, but I will not let others down. Now, I know that sounds terrible, but I find it's the case with a lot of my coaching clients, too. We put our own needs at the bottom of the pile, below kids, spouses, friends, parents, and even clients.

That's why oftentimes, building in accountability can mean ALL the difference between whether you will or will not...

- Write your book.
- Promote the webinar.
- Audition for a part.
- Actually do your exercise.
- Eat healthy.

- Learn a new skill.
- Finally run the 5k you always wanted to.
- Stop smoking.
- Go to a Toastmaster's meeting.
- Or really do any of the items on your bucket list.

Without accountability, it's too easy to just say "I'll get to that tomorrow" ... day after day after day and never ever end up reaching your goals.

The accountability can be public or private – but it just means having someone who you have to report to.

I have had personal experience both as the person who needed the accountability and the person coaching the person who needed the accountability.

I'll give you a few examples.

A few years back, I held the "Computer Butt Challenge" on my blog which was a 30 day challenge to see how many of my friends who were working in front of their computers day after day would join me in doing a bit of daily exercise.

The challenge motivated ME, since I was leading it, obviously, which is the reason I did it. I wanted to be held accountable to exercise for 30 days straight so I made it public on my blog and then I was "stuck" – in a good way. It also motivated a lot of my friends, especially on Fridays when we held the "Squat Off Challenge". Everyone started by doing 100 squats and then they posted how many they had done as the day went on. Someone would post 150 and the next person would post "Oh yeah, well I just did 160". There was a lot of friendly ribbing. Eventually the accountability and group mentality had people doing over 200 and 300 squats in one day – which was more than anyone thought they could do before the challenge. Yes, there were achy legs the next day, but it goes to show that public accountability and group support can bring up everyone together, including the leader – which in this case was me.

In the second example that I'd like to mention, I challenged myself. In 2010, I decided that I wanted to grow my exposure very rapidly, so my friend, Tracy Roberts and I brainstormed how I should do that.

The result? I decided to go on a "Blog World Tour" during the summer of that year. Every week, for 15 weeks, I would blog on a new site Monday through Friday, and then move on to another blog the next week. It totaled up to 75 blog posts and it kept me pretty busy.

But I did it. I had to. I promised all of my friends and people who I looked up to that their blog would be taken care of for an entire week during the summer, including that I would respond to comments and questions.

So, I was accountable to myself, I had also publicly announced my intentions, and I had promised 15 people in my industry that I would show up and do what I promised.

The results? I completed the tour and my business grew. When I showed up to conferences, people would run up to me and say "Oh my goodness. That was you on that blog!" It was pretty great.

For the third example that I'd like to share, again, I was the coach. My friend, Kristen Eckstein, who is a book publisher, came to me and said she was ready to "go big time" with her business. I said to her "Can you write and publish a high-quality book every week for the rest of this year?"

She said "Of course. It's what I do."

I said, "Ok. If you do it, it'll be huge for your credibility and exposure and we can make an event out of this that makes you totally stand out. BUT, despite sickness, holidays and other priorities you have to do it. If you don't achieve this, it'll make you look worse and not better, so are you sure?"

She said "Yes. Let's do it." And so she did. Through sickness, travel and life's interruptions, she published a new Kindle book every week for 18 weeks straight.

What was the magic in this instance?

1. She announced it publicly on her blog and to her audience.
2. She had me to report to every week, too.
3. She understood that this was a project that she had to get through and that at the end, she was done. I didn't ask her to write a book every week forever – just for a period of time.

It worked. And, at the end, she was able to take that momentum to teach a new Challenge of her own, the "Kindle in 30" challenge to help others to publish their books on Kindle.

I'd also like to talk about one of my favorite forms of accountability which is partnering on a project. Now, I don't advise partnering with someone without much forethought and consideration, but a partnership can be an amazing way to tie in accountability.

For instance, I have a business partner at a few parts of my business.

CoachGlue.com is a site that I co-created with my friend Melissa Ingold. We help coaches to create their own training with done-for-you programs. This helps other coaches to impact more people, make more money, and change more lives. It's a lot of fun, but I do know that every day, when I get on Skype, Melissa will be there and will be ready to move our business forward to reach OUR goals.

Beachpreneurs.com is another project that I have. This one is with my friend Kelly McCausey. We help entrepreneurs to live the lifestyle that they dream of. We focus on opening minds, challenging thoughts, and gathering smart awesome women at high-level mastermind retreats for amazing growth. Because of this partnership, I've got Kelly asking "what next" so this project also continues to grow at a quick clip, and we're constantly moving ahead.

Before you announce a challenge publicly – please make sure that you truly plan to follow through and you have contingencies built in. It doesn't matter if you get sick or have an emergency in your family. All people will remember if you miss your goal is that you didn't follow through.

That being said, if you set a goal, make sure it's one that you really will achieve. Don't plan to exercise EVERY DAY for a YEAR, but make it achievable like every day for a month, or 5 times a week for 90 days. Set yourself up to succeed, especially if it's a public challenge.

If you truly need help in an area, and you can't find people to help you to be accountable, then this is the time that you may need to hire a coach. Most of the people who you look up to have a coach to challenge them in one area of their lives. Whether it's a business coach, a personal trainer, a divorce coach, or even an accountability coach – find a way to make it happen. You deserve it.

Regret is something that none of us wants to face. I beg you to stop putting off your dreams in favor of business "busy". If you need someone to be accountable to, then face that and find someone. It's so much better than 10 years from now, still wishing that you'd reached your goals.

One last thing that I'd like to share about accountability is that the buddy system works really well, too. In 1999, my friend asked me to walk the Portland Marathon with her. Because it was her goal, too, I showed up for all of the training. We'd walk 20 miles every Saturday and several times during the week, too. I was not going to let her down so I ended up not letting ME down either.

Accountability is the gift that gives both ways.

Nicole Dean is the Mostly-Sane Marketer. (Ask anyone who knows her and they'll say that the "mostly" part is up for debate!) Her Mission: To Make Money and Build Businesses that Make the Web and the World a Better Place – and, Hopefully Have a Lot of Fun While Doing It. You can learn more about her at http://NicoleontheNet.com and http://Beachpreneurs.com

Chapter Four

Putting Your Stake in the Ground
By Kathleen Gage

"I've also learned that being accountable has more to do with my level of commitment to a life filled with purpose and meaning than just about anything."

In the 20 years I've had my business, I've learned a lot about accountability. Accountability to clients, my family and most of all to myself. If I were to sum it up in one phrase or thought, it would be about living one's truth.

Living our truth does not happen in one fell swoop. It can be a long, drawn-out process with many bumps in the road. My experience is such that just when I think I have it all figured out, I am given another opportunity to grow and to see how committed I am to my journey.

For as far back as I can remember, I dreamed of being a highly sought after public speaker. Today, speaking is a huge part of reaching my market and generating great revenues.

Yet, for many years I did nothing to move closer to the dream becoming manifest. For whatever reason, I just dreamed about being a speaker, but didn't take action on it.

Things began changing when I threw myself into learning anything and everything I could about setting and achieving goals. I went from thinking about what I wanted to taking action on my dreams.

It was when I was introduced to the works of Henry David Thoreau that I deeply understood it's not the giant leaps that get us on our path but rather the little steps that may seem insignificant that add up to giant leaps over the process of time.

If one advances confidently in the direction of one's dreams, and endeavors to live the life which one has imagined, one will meet with a success unexpected in common hours.

—Henry David Thoreau

Beginning in the eighties, I shifted from only thinking about being a professional speaker to dipping my toe in the water of my dream.

The speaking industry flourished through the eighties, and the greatest catalyst for my dream occurred in 1989 when I worked in the sales department of a small radio station in Santa Rosa, California.

I had successfully survived a decade-long period where not much seemed to work for me. At one point, due to poor choices, I ended up without a roof over my head, no job, no money and feeling as if the world were against me.

In the mid-eighties I discovered a world filled with possibilities—the self-help genre of books and cassette tapes. Delving deep into anything I could get my hands on, I learned a great deal about responsibility and accountability.

I discovered that all change came from within. For my outward circumstances to change, my thoughts and beliefs needed a major overhaul. From there, my actions absolutely needed to change.

Within a few short years, my life dramatically changed from one of drifting from day to day to securing my dream job at the radio station.

I went to work each day in a great state of mind, glad to be alive and to feel so good. My attitude was evident in all I did. I loved connecting clients with advertising campaigns that would grow their businesses, and I developed a solid client base of business owners who trusted my recommendations.

Although I enjoyed all of my clients, Ellen was my favorite. She was the marketing director for a large service station that employed over forty men and women. During one of my visits, Ellen and Scott, the owner of the business, excitedly introduced me to the works of Tony Robbins. Their excitement was contagious. Tony was impacting the lives of millions with his philosophy and teachings. He was taking the world by storm. They knew I would love his insights as much as they did.

Without hesitation I accepted their gift of *Personal Power: A 30-Day Program for Unlimited Success*. From the moment I popped in the first cassette tape, I was hooked. Like millions of others, my life went through a major shift when I not only listened to, but applied Tony Robbins's information. It was exactly what I needed. My life was moving in a great direction. I was confident about my future and about a life filled with possibility. That I felt so much hope for a great future was truly a miracle. I never dreamed that life could feel so good and that I had control over those feelings.

When Ellen and Scott realized how passionate I was about Tony Robbins's 30-day program, they presented me with an offer that would be a turning point on many levels. They said if I would go through the entire 30-day program, they would hire me to present my interpretation of the information to their staff.

Rather than pay cash, they offered to trade for $400 worth of services. At the time I was driving a car that had about 140,000 miles on it. It was in need of fairly constant repair. $400 in auto repairs was more than I could have asked for. I was in hog heaven. I felt like I had just been given the keys to the kingdom. That they offered me such a valuable trade for an hour presentation was a dream come true. I was living in a $200 per month studio in the bottom level of an older home. The living space totaled maybe 375 square feet— not much by most standards, but there had been a time when I had no place to call home, so it was a palace in my mind.

Ellen, Scott, and I sealed the deal with a handshake. I was stoked. I felt my life was really getting on the fast track to success. All the books I read, cassettes I listened to, goals I wrote down, and visions I had were beginning to show promise of something better. I put my heart and soul into creating my presentation.

Soon it became evident that I would actually be doing quite a bit of work for the $400 trade. Until I delved into the project, I had no idea what it entailed. During the day I listened to Tony Robbins's cassettes as I drove to and from appointments with clients. At night I feverishly prepared my presentation. Was I nervous? Yes. It was not because of the presentation itself, but because I wanted to give them the very best I could in return for their trust.

After a week I began to have serious doubts about my ability to deliver. I was overcome with fear. What was I thinking? Not long before, I had had no job, no home, no self-respect, and no money to my name. What made me think I could inspire others to live a more productive life? The more my self-talk increased, the more I felt like a complete phony. A part of me wanted to run away and not look back. How could I have been so stupid as to think I could ever turn my life around?

I called a close friend to share my thoughts and doubts. She listened patiently as I expressed my doubts. After listening to me dump my emotions on her for a few minutes, she calmly gave me reasons why I didn't need to beat myself up.

Our reality changes with our willingness to do things differently. We get into patterns of behavior that are familiar and comfortable to the point of limitation. In order to change our thinking, our beliefs, and our reality, we have to be willing to go through some discomfort. We have to reject our black-and-white thinking. Gloria pointed out that I didn't need to be perfect in my delivery, nor did I have to measure up to the Tony Robbinses of the world. I simply had to take one step in the right direction and share something of value. She also pointed out I had made a commitment and not to follow through was not the responsible thing to do.

What a revelation! We don't have to have everything figured out from the very beginning! The process of success is an unfolding. It is a step-by-step process. Put one foot in front of the other and keep moving.

How often have you held yourself back from trying something new because you didn't have it all figured out yet? But when your back is against the wall, you will figure out the best solution.

If we are to grow, change, and become more of who we are meant to be, we have to be willing to walk through the unknown, the discomfort, and the confusion to get to the other side. Our lives are created moment-by-moment, decision-by-decision. We don't come into this world with everything figured out. We have to be willing to stumble, fall, get up, and try again and again until we achieve our outcome. Something that was a challenge when we first began often becomes second nature the longer and the more we do it.

When I prepared my presentation for Ellen and Scott's team, I wondered if it would always be that difficult. Not only are such presentations now a regular part of what I do, but also what took me weeks and weeks back then is second nature now. Why? Because I now have decades of experience.

When the big day arrived, I was beside myself with excitement. My goal was to make it an incredible experience for everyone attending. All the while I just knew this was the first step in my life's true journey. The evening went off without a hitch. Everyone loved the presentation. I had done an incredibly good job. Ellen was beyond happy and Scott said it was one of the best presentations he had ever heard. Wow! I was better than I ever dreamed I would be. I was a natural, and felt I could just about write my own ticket. This was what I was destined to do. But my immediate future offered up a serving of humble pie. Shortly afterward, Scott's father approached me to compliment me on my presentation. Completely filled with ego, I was being set up for "Pride goeth before the fall."

"You are amazing!" he began. "I would love for you to do the same presentation tomorrow night for another group. I don't have the budget for it, but it will give you more experience," he said as he waited for my response.

"Absolutely! I would love to," I quickly responded.

Without asking anything about the people I would be speaking to, I was given the time and location for the presentation. The following day I had a difficult time containing my excitement. Even though it was a cold and rainy day, I felt as if the sun were shining wherever I went. In between client visits I fantasized about what my life could be like if all I did was go from location to location to motivate and inspire people.

At the appointed time, I drove to the facility. It didn't take long to notice that many of the attendees were in a really bad mood. They were soaking wet from the rain and they were dressed very differently from the group the night before. They were in mud-splattered overalls, jeans, sweatshirts, and work boots. These were tow truck drivers, and there was a lot of rude and obscene conversation going on, and beer-guzzling contests followed by encouragements to see who could belch the loudest. I felt the separation between me and the new group growing wider by the minute.

Here I was in a pressed business suit, carrying a briefcase, and wearing high heels. The differences became more apparent by the minute. 'What in the world was I thinking? Why would I even think I could do this for a living? Who do you think you are?" were the type of questions swelling in my mind.

By the time I was introduced with a short "This woman is going to motivate you to do more with your life," it was apparent that my experience that evening would be very, very different from that of the previous one. Within moments of taking the stage, the boos and hisses began.

"Get that woman out of here," one drunken audience member yelled. I felt like finding the first rock I could crawl under and pretending I was in a bad dream.

I was devastated. Doing what I could to contain my composure, it felt like an eternity before I was done. An incredible feeling of defeat overtook me on the drive home. That was all it took for me to resolve never to try public speaking again. "I don't ever want to do this for a living. This sucks." The self-talk started again: "Who do you think you are to think you could do this? Look at where you come from. Who would want to learn anything from you? Why don't you just accept the fact that you are a loser?"

In one short twenty-four hour period my speaking career began and ended. What I failed to realize during the shortest speaking career in history was that it would take work to be successful at it.

My old way of thinking was creeping in. Thinking I had it all figured out and didn't need to put much effort into public speaking had put me in this situation. If anything were to change, I had to be willing to change my thinking and my actions.

It is when we change our thinking and actions that life does change. It was necessary to feel the pain, learn from the experience and decide how committed I was to my dream.

I nearly let that one defeat determine the course of my life. Fortunately, my desire to live my dream was greater than my fear of criticism.

After over a decade invested in self-development through books, tapes, workshops, and spiritual teachings, my thinking was night and day to what it had been. I had a job I loved in the marketing department at GTE, and I felt like I had enough evidence to prove that with commitment, vision, and perseverance, virtually anything is possible. The difference this time around was knowing that I needed to gain the knowledge about how to do it. There were steps that needed to be taken. I couldn't shortcut my way to success.

Previously I had wanted something fast and without the effort of building a foundation and gaining the appropriate knowledge and training. My life reflected this attitude, with lackluster results. I call it the "easy button" mentality.

The "easy button" mentality is prevalent throughout our culture. I see this a great deal with people who want to start a business. Many think that if they buy one book, that is all it will take for them to have instant success.

I was incredibly guilty of this type of thinking, but over the years my thinking has taken on a complete 180-degree turn... for the better, I might add.

What I've learned is there are specific things I need to do to ensure my success, regardless of what I want to succeed at, and it will likely take longer than expected.

I've also learned that being accountable has more to do with my level of commitment to a life filled with purpose and meaning than just about anything. Today, I make a great living working with entrepreneurs who know they are here to make a difference. More times than not, we work on their level of commitment to their dream.

I often find myself smiling when I realize the life I am living is a direct result of being willing to hold myself accountable to living a life filled with meaning. The greatest joy I get is in sharing my journey with those who know they are here to do something amazing. Had I not held myself accountable to my dreams my life would be very different from what it is.

I likely would still be someone who blamed people, places and things for a life with little passion. But instead of that road, I chose the road of putting my stake in the ground and knowing, no matter what, if I was willing to do what it takes, be accountable and live with integrity, life would be better than I ever imagined.

Kathleen Gage is the "no-nonsense, common sense" online marketing strategist, speaker, author, product creation specialist, and owner of Power Up For Profits. She helps entrepreneurs make money online. Her clients are driven by making a difference through their own unique voice.

As an early adopter of online marketing, Kathleen is considered to be one of the nation's most passionate speakers. She is known for cutting through the fluff and helping people leave their sob stories behind so they can stop focusing on the past and start looking towards the future. She speaks and teaches about what she believes are the core elements of a successful life: accountability, integrity, honesty, and living with passion and hope.

Chapter Five

Accountability – Where's the Fun In That?
By Paul Taubman

"When you are personally accountable for your actions (especially as part of an accountability group), you are stating that you are taking ownership of situations that you are part of."

"My philosophy is that not only are you responsible for your life, but doing the best at this moment puts you in the best place for the next moment."

- Oprah Winfrey

Responsible and **Responsibility** always sound like "grown-up" terms. To me it seems to have a negative connotation. Even though most people would say I am an adult and I am 'responsible,' it takes the child-like wonder out of the things we do. After all, a child is not necessarily 'responsible' so how can we have fun doing the things we want to do if we have to be responsible and all grown up?

What is all this talk about responsibility when you are expecting to hear about accountability? It has been my experience that people relate the two words together. If you are accountable, you are responsible. And you can be responsible for your actions when you are accountable.

But what does all this mean? Before I answer that, let me tell you who I am and why you should read any further. My name is Paul B. Taubman, II and I am the founder of the website   http://INeedHelpWithWordPress.com   and http://AllAboutGratitude.com - I have been getting more things accomplished than most of the people I know. I have a full time job, a very successful website training business, I am an author, an international speaker, I run the local cable tv station, I volunteer for several charitable organizations, I teach at a college, I travel, and I have a lot of fun. I do this all in the same amount of time that you have available to do the things you want to do.

How can I get all of this done when some people say they don't have enough time to even watch the latest episode of some XYZ Reality show? The answer is simple – I get held accountable.

For me, accountability is a tool that I use to get more things done. Do you need to get more accomplished? The key secret to getting everything done is to let people know about it. I am grateful to a select group of friends that hold me accountable when I tell them about things I need to do.

That does not mean that you should run out and tell everyone your hopes and dreams. There are many dream killers out there (I certainly know more than a few people like that – there were many of them in my family!)

No, don't tell everyone about what you want to accomplish, but pick select people that get excited when you talk about what you want to do. These are the special people in your life that cheer you on and help you to the finish-line – not the people who may unintentionally hold you back.

You know the two types of people. Tell someone you want to write a book and they say, "Wow! Really? That is a lot of work. Wouldn't you rather go play basketball tonight instead?" Or, you might get a comment like, "You? Write a book? Don't make me laugh!" Or it might even be a less subtle remark such as, "If you write a book, you then have to market it. You don't want to do that."

On the other hand, you can get comments back like, "That is great! Want me to proofread it as you go along?" Or someone says, "What a coincidence! My neighbor works at a publisher – maybe I can get you some info on what needs to be done!"

One group wants to knock you down and the other wants to bring you up. You may have enough difficulties along the way on your own; there is no need to purposefully get knocked around by all the naysayers! You want to hang around those that will lift you up and support you in your efforts.

Personally, I have been part of a mastermind group for over 8 years. The great success leader, Napoleon Hill, created the concept almost 80 years ago with his book, Think and Grow Rich. If you are not familiar with the term, a mastermind group is designed to help you get through challenges using the collective intelligence of the other members in your mastermind

My small group of friends are there for the sole purpose of helping each other out. Every week we get on a phone call and discuss where we are with our goals, our progress, our setbacks, and our successes. Each week the four of us provide positive feedback and constructive criticism to each other. In some cases, we encourage one another to push a little further.

What makes this so powerful is that towards the end of each call we provide our goals for the following week. The following week, we hold each other accountable for what we said we would do. If my goal or challenge for the week is to develop a new information product, I know I better do it! I want to get it done because I know that I told them that I would.

When you let people know that you are going to do something, there is a part of you that does not want to let you go back and proclaim, "I didn't get that done." You want to live up to your word – you said you were going to do something, so you want to accomplish it.

Even though I have my mastermind to help me with things in addition to accountability (only a small part of the mastermind's benefit is the accountability), I have had different accountability partners through the years. In some cases it was a one-on-one basis. It was me and another person. We would have short touch point meetings every morning when we were each working on a deadline. Again, I could have gotten to the end by myself (maybe...) but knowing that I would have to get on the phone in the morning and provide that status helped me keep to my plan and even surpass it!

In another Accountability Group I belong to, I was very lackadaisical in my participation. I was not accountable at all and my progress showed. There were a few factors that precluded me from participating to the fullest, and I have no one to blame but myself. The moment I bumped up a notch and made the time and effort to be accountable to the group, my overall productivity on this project went through the roof!

Sometimes we just need to learn the hard way. And it is usually the simple things that we already know that we need to relearn. I know the value of an accountability partner or group, yet I ignored it. I knew I would suffer and I chose not to participate. What happened? I suffered!

In that sense, accountability is like exercise. We know we need it and that we should do it. Studies have shown that if you exercise more, you become more productive and actually get 'time back.' Yet we make excuses like, "I don't have time."

When you are personally accountable for your actions (especially as part of an accountability group), you are stating that you are taking ownership of situations that you are part of. You let your group know that you are going to take the actions needed to complete whatever the task at hand is and just as important, you state that you will see them through, and you take responsibility for what happens – good or bad. You don't blame others if things go wrong. Instead, you do your best to make things right.

Personal integrity comes shining through when you are held accountable for what you say you are going to do.

There will be times when you commit to complete a task yet it goes unfinished. There is nothing to be ashamed of for not accomplishing your goal. There may be some very good reasons why it was not completed – you ran out of time, the goal was a big and lofty one and was not possible, you were reliant on someone or something else that was not available, or maybe the task simply was no longer a priority. All of these reasons are acceptable and a good group will help provide some alternative ideas to complete the task. In some cases, it may be wise to simply revise your goals for the following week.

Here is the bottom line... As my father used to mimic the television commercial, "Try it, you'll like it!" If you have never been in an accountability group or a mastermind, try one out. See if it is something that will work for you. See if it will help increase your productivity. See if it helps you accomplish the tasks at hand that you have been procrastinating about.

And when you see all those things occur, you will stick with it and have fun doing it.

Paul B. Taubman, II is an expert trainer. Travelling across the county, Paul trained countless folks how to work on intricate computer systems. He was a Master Trainer teaching Instructors across the country how to teach courses. As a highly respected College Adjunct, Paul teaches technical Computer Programming courses.

With all this training experience, Paul has learned how to teach all this "technical stuff" to non-techies! He is a master at taking the obscure and complex and explaining it in a simple, fun, and educational way.

Paul teaches entrepreneurs how to make money with their website.

Your stress levels will melt away after working with Paul as you take control of your website and turn it into a profit machine. Visit http://INeedHelpWithWordPress.com for more information.

Chapter Six

Three Tips for Accountability Success
By Birgitta Jorgenson

"To me, an accountability coach is an objective observer who is looking from the outside in, staying with you remotely as you travel along your journey."

Are you enjoying the stories you have read so far? Hopefully you are highlighting or taking notes for quick reference later. There is much that can be gained by learning from a group of people and comparing the variety of perspectives that have been presented! My name is Birgitta Jorgenson and I am happy to provide further insight into my experience with an accountability coach and the success I've had so far, as well as offering a few tips to help you prepare for inviting an accountability coach into your life.

To start, I am an entrepreneur who has been working on a new approach to "traditional" education. My story begins in the fall of 2009, when I made the conscious decision to move forward with an idea I had thought up back in the mid 1990's. I spent a full year organizing my thoughts and getting every detail down on paper. By 2011, I was officially the Founder and Visionary for Irblich Schools, in the eyes of the IRS. I decided to start this journey by using my greatest strengths of being a strategic thinker outside of what is usually expected in the childcare industry, as well as tapping into my skills of digging for research and organizing the findings into procedures and processes. With my degree in Early Childhood Education, I embarked on the first steps of this big goal by launching a holistic preschool.

My introduction to the idea of an accountability coach began when I joined a mastermind group which met biweekly. I was with this group for a couple of years and became very proficient at making sure that the goals I set were either accomplished or at least attempted before attending each meeting. I find that when you verbally commit to doing something and then have to report your results later in front of a close knit group of your peers, that is basically what being accountable for your actions is all about. At the mastermind gatherings, each member decided what they wanted to accomplish by the next meeting, and I was always careful to make sure that the goals were not too simple or the other extreme, impossible. The idea is to have several small successes that each lead you closer and closer to the big end goal. The really great thing about your end goal is that, as time goes by on your journey, it will change or adjust. Fortunately for me, during the time I was participating in the mastermind group, I was able to easily assess what was already in my schedule for the next two weeks and how much time I could devote to each task. As a side note, being in a group like this really improved my time management skills.

Let's take a look at how I incorporated accountability into a specific project of mine. To give you some background, there was a business contest being hosted by a well known international magazine and each week a new challenge would be posted online for the participants to do and then they would report back their results on the magazine's blog. Reading and responding to other business owners was, in itself, a very rewarding experience. I gained two wonderful long-distant connections through that experience which I still maintain today. Everyone participating was indirectly keeping the other participants accountable, even if there was a bit of friendly competition involved. But I'm getting ahead of myself. Before I began this business contest adventure, I asked the mastermind mentor and one other member to be my accountability partners. I decided two would be better than one, especially knowing that each of them had their own lives and if one wasn't available I could always count on the other. Each week I would share the presented challenge to both ladies as well as my results before submitting them publically online. This extra step also meant I couldn't wait until the last minute to complete the assignments. One of the things I liked about this accountability arrangement was how they would both question and sometimes debate what I had done. It would make me think beyond my own ideas. Occasionally I would find the final results would even surprise me, and once or twice I started an assignment over again from scratch because between the three of us it would be decided I could approach the challenge from a better angle. Other times I found that, through our discussions, I was able to better clarify my own thoughts. The whole experience was very positive and rewarding.

I never had intended to win this online business contest because at the time it was running, my preschool was not open yet. This made some of the weekly challenges very difficult, as I needed to speculate upon the potential results since I had no clients, employees or actual financials to refer to. However, because I was working with my accountability partners, I was able to see the entire business contest through to the end and as a result, had an amazing document to reference when my business was ready to launch. I was never allowed to say, "I'll do it later" when working with my accountability partners. As well, having verbally announced what I was doing, I wasn't allowed to quit because somebody would always be checking in periodically and asking how things were going.

So here is your first tip: <u>accountability can be as simple as writing something down and then sharing it with someone,</u> such as a family member or friend. The key to remember here is that the goal you are seeking needs to have some way for both you and others to measure whether or not you achieved the desired outcome.

I will forever be grateful for all the mastermind participants I had the pleasure of collaborating with and especially my accountability coach, Debbie O'Grady, who I hired again during the year that Irblich Schools opened. She made sure I didn't get lost working only in the day-to-day operations of my business, but also continued to encourage me to allocate time to work on the bigger picture for the business as well.

One of the best techniques that my accountability coach used was asking me reflective questions when things did not go as planned. She would listen carefully to what I said, and even observe how I said it, both in tone and through my body language. Was I self-sabotaging? Did I plan poorly? Had I invited the right people to help? Or maybe I was trying to do everything by myself without asking for help at all! Was there something I could learn from the experience so that it can be avoided next time?

To me, an accountability coach is an objective observer who is looking from the outside in, staying with you remotely as you travel along your journey. This type of coach can offer occasional course corrections so that you hit your target on the bulls-eye, or at least right next to it. I feel confident enough to say that you will have better odds with a coach than without. The reason for this is because a coach does not get easily clouded with all the emotions, stories or lies we have swirling around in our heads. They are able to see those reoccurring and sometimes destructive patterns. By making us aware of these patterns, we are able to better achieve our desired goals.

Here is your second important tip if you want to work with an accountability coach: <u>you need to make a commitment</u>. To really benefit, there needs to be a relationship for at least one year to see results. I think it would be difficult to figure out any sort of pattern in less than a year. For some strange reason, people tend to live behind a mask, typically for 2-3 months when in new surroundings, and sometimes even longer. Let me give you an example that many of you may be able to relate to. When couples first start dating, both individuals are usually looking their best and acting on their best behavior. When the relationship gets to the stage of living together, whether married or not, more of each person's true identity starts to be revealed, including habits. Did each person in the relationship change? No! Although it may seem that way, it is because we begin to feel more comfortable around the other person and we act more like who we truly are. This behavior is how our culture deals with this unusual yet common personality quirk. And it is for this reason that I recommend working with an accountability coach for at least a year, so that the coach really has an opportunity to observe, get to know you, and hopefully support you. Whatever the accountability coach helps you realize about yourself, it will become useful as you move forward with each new project in the future.

Let's say you really want to take a product or service to the next level in your industry. In this case I would suggest putting the idea of your friends and family aside and highly recommend hiring a reputable accountability coach instead. Having an unrelated third party ask you if you did what you said you were going to do is very powerful and surprisingly motivating. Try to finding a coach by asking people you already know for referrals. If you have to sign a contract, make sure there is some sort of clause to cancel without any further financial obligation, so that you can find out if your personality clashes too much with theirs. Remember, this coach may not become your best friend, but if you don't like or respect them, then it will be very difficult to listen to them when they have to tell you some hard truths. Even with a coach that you like, debating with them is one thing, but becoming defensive is another and not acceptable or professional behavior. Be warned... the coach will likely have to ask you some questions that will make you uncomfortable. Chances are high that you will benefit the most when you can get through that uncomfortable process. Another way you could experience what it would be like to work with an accountability coach is to see if they would be willing to do a small project with you so that you can try them out before bringing them on for a bigger project. Sort of like taking a vehicle for a test drive. From a business point of view, find out how they handle bumps, heavy traffic or scenic detours?

I realize I have spent some time on how to choose an accountability coach, but let's not forget that this is a two way street.

Here is my third and final tip: <u>You must be coachable, which means you need to be open to hearing suggestions and other points of view.</u> If you have something very specific in mind and you are not willing to budge for any reason, then the accountability coach may still agree to be there for you, but you may also be losing out on an opportunity for a great alliance or advocate for your product or service. My experience has been that even when I feel I have a great idea, once I finally decide to share it with someone else, they always seem to have a little something to add. Just like adding spice to a recipe to bring it from bland to grand, so too goes the collaboration of minds. There is no rule saying that you have to follow the suggestions that your accountability coach or others give you, but at least have the courtesy to consider their ideas and give a valid reason why you would not incorporate the suggestions. Remember, this process might help clarify for each of you the direction that is trying to be reached.

I hope you found my personal experience with accountability helpful. As a quick review, the three tips I would offer to help guide you towards success, especially if you are considering hiring an accountability coach, would be: 1) make sure your goals are written down and results can be measured, 2) plan to make a commitment for at least one year, or until a specific project is completed, and 3) you absolutely must be coachable. A little resilience in this department will do everyone involved some good.

A goal is only a target waiting to be hit, and a coach
can align your aim towards the bull's eye!
                              ~Birgitta Jorgenson~

Wishing you success in attaining both big and small goals.

Birgitta Jorgenson was born and raised in Canada. After moving to the United States, she was quickly discouraged by the

Florida childcare system and found herself popping in and out of her chosen career. Then life presented a different plan. Birgitta had kept notes at each job held. It was time to take those notes and organize them in preparation to launch an alternative approach to education that was more in alignment with the universe. But first, Birgitta needed to become more business savvy. She thrust herself into the direct sales industry for the best hands-on education. Birgitta learned many skills, including the value of networking and the power of collaboration. She is honored to contribute a chapter to this book, and hopes that others will be inspired to follow their dreams. "But don't forget..." Birgitta notes, "...remember to stop, breath, listen and observe along the way. There just might be a subtle message waiting for you with a much bigger dream than you could have ever imagined!" http://IrblichSchools.com

Chapter Seven

The Trials, Tribulations and Successes of Accountability
By Adrienne Dupree

"According to dictionary.com, accountable means being responsible to someone or being responsible for some action. In my experience, accountability has been given a bad reputation or a "bad rep"."

Who Is Adrienne Dupree?

When I am asked to tell you who I am, I have to say I am probably much different than people perceive me to be. I was born in Washington, DC, grew up in the Washington DC suburbs and am a 3rd generation Washingtonian. That in itself is odd. Most people are transplants to Washington, DC. I originally started my college career as a Political Science major but changed to Mathematics and Electrical Engineering. I started my professional career as a Software Engineer, working my way up to a Program Manager. I am a government contractor or as we are affectionately called in the Washington, DC area, "Beltway Bandits". Even though I have been in corporate America my entire career, I have had several entrepreneurial endeavors. I had a wedding invitation business at one time, was a part-time Mortgage Broker and even participated in several network marketing companies.

I stumbled upon online marketing and it was congruent with my technical background. The Online Newbie was created and its mission is to help people in corporate America who want to start an online marketing business.

Accountability and Its Woes

According to dictionary.com, accountable means being responsible to someone or being responsible for some action. In my experience, accountability has been given a bad reputation or a "bad rep". For example, in the corporate world, accountability is often associated with negative behavior or consequences. When you hear someone say, "You need to hold him accountable", it is usually associated with a person that has not completed a task that they should have completed. It is also associated with punishment as opposed to looking at it in a positive way. I think this is why people shy away from accountability and don't believe that it can be useful or helpful.

I don't see accountability in this negative light. I see it as an opportunity for someone to shine and actually do what they say they are going to do. If I say that I am going to complete a task by a certain time, then I need to hold myself accountable and complete the task on time. Accountability cannot be a one way street. You need to be accountable as well as hold others accountable for tasks.

My Personal Experiences With Accountability

I have had many personal experiences with accountability in both my corporate career, my personal life as well as in my online business. As a Program Manager, I am responsible for ensuring that my programs deliver on time and within budget. I am not the one actually executing all of the work, so I have to depend on my team to actually get the work done. The way that I like to work is to sit down with my team and determine when the work can actually be accomplished. There are times, though, when we have specific deadlines so then we need to come up with solutions on how we can meet the deadline. When my staff is actually involved in coming up with the deadlines, it is much easier to hold them accountable for the dates and the completion of the work. They were a part of the decision and have actually created the deadlines.

In my online business, one way I practice accountability is by having an Accountability Partner. This is someone that I communicate with on a regular basis about the things I am doing and plan to do in my business. I find that this works best if the tasks or "promises" are actually written down. At the beginning of each week, you write down the tasks you are going to accomplish for the week and send it to your Accountability Partner. You go over the tasks for the week and the tasks you were to complete the week before. Every day, you either talk on the phone or send an email to let your partner know if you accomplished the previous day's goals and what you plan to do that day. This is very effective because you don't want to have to tell your partner that you did not get your goals completed. If you do not complete your tasks, you feel like you have let your partner down.

Another example of where I am using accountability is to obtain my Project Manager Professional certification or PMP. I have been dragging my feet about studying and preparing for this test. I have formed an accountability group with two of my co-workers. We have a schedule of what is to be accomplished every week. We meet on Sundays to review and study together. Since I am not that motivated to prepare for this test, this will definitely help. I will make sure I keep up because I don't want to let my group down. Hopefully, this accountability group will keep me on track and help me reach my goal.

I also used accountability while raising my son. Parents these days have the tendency to be overly involved in the school work, homework and projects assigned to their children. As he became older, I made a conscious decision that I would no longer stay up all night to help him complete projects when he waited to the last minute to complete them. I was supportive but would no longer enable him. He needed to be accountable for his decisions and accept the consequences for his actions.

In general, I hold myself accountable for things that I need to do. I am not perfect and sometimes it is easier said than done to be accountable. The goal is to get back on the right track when things go awry.

How To Make Accountability Work

I think that, in order for accountability to actually be successful in a work environment, both parties need to participate in setting the goals or expectations. If the manager is just telling the employee that a certain task needs to be done by a specific time, then the outcome may not be favorable. If the expectation is that a task will be completed on time, then the employee needs to have some input into what the task entails as well as the due date. Both parties need to have "skin in the game". If this is more of a participatory exercise, then I believe it is received much better.

In order for an accountability partnership to work, both parties need to take their commitments seriously. In the case of accountability partners, you are operating as peers instead of a boss employee relationship. You need to be able to call your partner on the carpet when you see a pattern of missed tasks. This can be difficult to do depending on your personality and the relationship you have with your partner. The whole idea of this partnership is to help each other succeed and actually be as productive as possible.

Parting Advice

My parting advice to you is that you should consider having an Accountability Partner. If you have tasks that you need to complete that are falling behind, an accountability partner may be your saving grace. You may not think you need or can benefit from one and that is exactly how I felt in the beginning. I hold myself personally accountable for the things I know I need to accomplish so I was not sure how beneficial this would be. I am pretty self-motivated and have always been able to complete tasks and goals. I was not that keen on the whole idea of having an Accountability Partner in the beginning. I am an introvert so the idea of that much interaction was a little unnerving. It turned out to be a great experience and I encourage everyone to try it. Even if you are a self-starter having an Accountability Partner is just "icing on the cake".

When you are thinking about incorporating accountability into your life, you need to make sure you are not using it as a means of punishment. You want to make this a positive experience. I am a strong believer that if parents start early on to make their children accountable for their decisions and actions, they will grow up to be productive citizens that can take care of themselves.

Adrienne Dupree is a full-time Program Manager for a government contractor, an author and a part-time online marketer. She has a technical background with a B.S. Mathematics, B.S. Electrical Engineering and M.S. Computer Science. Her company, The Online Newbie, is for people in corporate America who want to get out the rat race, stop trading time for dollars and be in control of their own destiny so that they can start an online marketing business. She is well equipped to really help this audience because she is part of this community. She understands the pressures of having a demanding corporate full time job and how to balance it with a part-time online marketing business. To find out more about Adrienne Dupree and how you can leave the corporate world behind go to http://www.leavethecorporateworldbehind.com

Chapter Eight

Accountability Partnering for Success
By Kathi Laughman

"Accountability is not about answering to someone else's wants or desires. It isn't measuring up to someone else's expectations. It is about staying committed to your own dreams and taking productive actions."

In November of 2005 my personal life changed with a shower of rice. I went from being a single Mom after 23 years to joining the ranks of single empty nesters. Three years later, in January of 2009 my professional life was changed by a pink slip. I left the ranks of the executive suite to join the throngs of the unemployed in tough economic times. Keeping pace, three years later in 2012 both my personal and professional life changed again sitting in a doctor's office. My health was demanding immediate and total attention. I'm sure you would agree that each of these moments were worthy of being called disruptive. And even when predictable, any change at a level that disrupts the ebb and flow of our daily life has an all-encompassing impact.

Those years served as a university of life. In each case, I was faced with the choice of either being diminished or inspired by what was happening in my life. I chose to be inspired. But it was not easy. Because change is hard, especially when you actually liked things the way they were!

Why am I sharing this with you? Because choosing to be inspired by the events in my life was not due to any great personal wisdom. It was the result of a powerful relationship that started in the midst of all of this with a life coach. I did not know anything about life coaching before I hired one. Through some serendipitous events, I ended up on the website of Nightingale Conant and took one of their surveys. Part of that service was a session with one of their life coaches. I had no idea, on that afternoon, what an impact that exercise was going to have on my future.

As I went through a personal development program under the expert guidance of my life coach, I fell in love with the process of coaching. It was as if everything I had ever done personally and professionally now melded together into a whole that put all of that experience to work serving others.

The page was effectively turned for the next chapter of my life.

My next step was to do something with this new direction. I created my own economy by starting my own business and coaching practice. My coaching programs focus in three areas. The first covers mindset, motivation and method. It's how we accomplish anything. It is about perspective, positioning and performance. And it's simply called our M3 program. It is developing you to your highest power.

The second program addresses the area of strategy, which is where you benefit from the 25+ years I spent creating strategic plans for hundreds of companies, departments, projects and products. The focus here is a life plan that is delivered daily through your action plan.

Third is the Wisdom Well program where the focus is on your community and network; where you serve and are served. It does in fact take a village to raise ourselves – but not just any village!

In each of these programs, one of the key elements of the coaching relationship is accountability. It is an essential part of the partnership. One of my favorite insights comes from Ralph Waldo Emerson when he said this: "Our chief want in life is somebody who will make us do what we can." That is the essence of coaching for me and beautifully explains how accountability plays into the relationship.

We've all had the experience of good intentions that fall by the wayside. Life happens. We get busy and lose focus. Each time this is our experience, our belief in our dreams, even in ourselves, diminishes. Over time, that can lead to a life that is so much less than our potential. That only changes when we take responsibility for our lives by taking ownership of our decisions and their consequences, good and bad.

The role of the coach as an accountability partner is to keep the light shining so brightly on our desired path that we cannot help but stay on track. Taking an example from my work within the field of supply chain logistics, this is like building what we call a geo-fence on our path to success. When moving goods from point A to point B where the route is critical, we build an electronic fence on the route that is monitored by satellites that will use GPS technologies to keep track of the goods along the way. If the truck goes outside of that route, alarms start going crazy! Right away, the people that need to know are alerted that the truck is not on track and everyone works together to get those goods headed back in the right direction. An accountability plan and coaching relationship works very much the same.

A goal is set and a strategy is defined for reaching it. That is like the route to the destination. We then create check-in points that serve just like that geo-fence along the way. The coach uses agreed technologies to monitor how the client is progressing along the way. If they start to go off-track, the coach can recognize that they need to step in and help them get back on the right road so that they can reach their end goal. The key is that it must be about helping you achieve your goals.

Accountability is not about answering to someone else's wants or desires. It isn't measuring up to someone else's expectations. It is about staying committed to your own dreams and taking productive actions. Accountability can be, and quite often is, what makes the difference in whether or not we reach our goals. It is the glue that holds our resolve together as we navigate to the successful attainment of those goals.

Why does accountability make such a difference? Because sometimes the most challenging person to manage is ourselves! An accountability partner forces us to accept complete transparency and feedback for the reality of what is working and what isn't. Quite often we cannot see for ourselves where our habits or reflex responses learned over time are hindering our progress. Being challenged to stay the course brings all of that into focus as well.

In my own life, having an accountability partner has created benefits for me with my health, my finances and my professional goals. The most recent has been working with a health coach. Together, we designed an overall plan for my well-being that I execute daily. Part of the plan covers nutrition.

For accountability, I maintain an electronic food log and record calories and other key nutrition information. My coach has access to that log. When I take a detour, she's right there checking in with me to see what's going on and suggesting a plan to get me back on track. Another part is a pedometer tool I wear that is tracking my steps and movement. Each day I have a goal to reach and it tells me where I am at to that goal throughout the day. The tool itself is an accountability partner. Since hydration is such a core component of our overall well-being, that is another activity we agreed to track. The food eaten, how much water I consumed and how many steps I take every day are recorded and reported. Even when I am alone, knowing that someone else is seeing what I'm doing electronically helps to keep me in check. There is no hiding the truth of the reality of my actions. So there can be no excuses.

That brings me to what I believe are the five key essentials to making accountability work for you in achieving your goals.

1. Start with the goal. You must begin with the end in mind.
2. Determine 3 – 5 key actions or activities that are going to have the greatest impact.
3. Do an honest assessment for where you are now in these key areas to create your baseline for moving forward.
4. Set incremental milestones along the way for each action or activity that require you to stretch

but are reasonable so that if you need to adjust you can.

5.   Determine the most effective way to track your ACTIONS and your PROGRESS in each key area.

Once you have stepped through each of these five points, you can leverage accountability to energize and empower you to achieve any goal you set for yourself with enthusiasm and ease.

My final point focuses on the selection of tools you will use as part of your accountability partnership plan. In the personal example I've provided, the accountability tools are just as important as my coach. Make it easy to record and track what you do (or do not do!). Wherever possible, make the reporting of that tied to how you're recording it. In today's world, it's never been easier to create real time, full disclosure of our actions and results. Leverage the power of that to propel you forward as you move to the successful achievement of your goals.

Kathi Laughman is a best-selling author, inspirational speaker, certified life coach and strategist. She is the founder and CEO of The Mackenzie Circle LLC, a life coaching and personal leadership company where she champions her clients as their possibility partner, coach, and mentor.

Kathi's personal mission is to inspire, facilitate, and invest in the success of others. Learn more at www.MackenzieCircle.com.

Chapter Nine

But It's Conventional Wisdom, It Must Be Right! By Geoff Hoff

> *"I was unwilling to write that nightly [accountability] email and have to admit I hadn't accomplished everything I'd promised. Better to just get the stuff done."*

When I was younger, I heard that, if you need motivation from outside yourself, you're doing something wrong. It was part of the spirit of this country in the fifties and sixties; rugged individuals doing it on their own, not relying on anyone but themselves in a plucky stance of confident productivity. It was part of the Protestant Work Ethic that we all must adhere to whether we are Protestant or not.

Being accountable to yourself was noble and worthwhile. Relying on someone else was a recipe for disaster and proof you were weak and somehow incomplete. Actually needing someone else to help you be accountable for your actions was even worse, a major character flaw. If you needed help getting motivated, or getting anything done, there was something intrinsically wrong with you on some basic level and you'd better pull yourself up by your own bootstraps, put your nose to the grindstone, place one foot in front of the other and other mixed metaphors and annoying clichés.

There is some merit to all that, I suppose, especially if there is no one you can rely on, but mostly, I've come to think it's poppycock mixed with a healthy dose of horse pucky.

I kind of took it on most of my younger life, though, and got support for that kind of thinking by a lot of the "human potential" stuff I read at the time. I got stuff done, but I spent a lot of time spinning my wheels and feeling alone and unsupported. I'm a writer, have written since I was a kid. In my early thirties, I wrote a project with another writer. Having a writing partner was a completely different experience from what I was used to. The writing flowed in a whole new way. What we wrote together was completely distinct from what I wrote by myself. That first writing partnership (and the second) faded away for reasons having nothing to do with the writing, but in the late nineties, I worked on an episodic stage show playing in Los Angeles just off Hollywood Boulevard. One of the other writers on the show suggested we work together on an episode and we realized very quickly that we loved working together.

This writing partnership stuck (with the usual ups and downs of any relationship, of course, but the writing, ultimately, was more important than any issue or conflict.) We started working together on other projects, then became good friends. We read each other's work, stuff we'd written on our own. One day, we decided we'd make promises to each other about how many pages we'd write on our own before the next time we got together for our next joint writing session. I wrote more short stories in that period than at any other time before or since. I didn't want to get to the next writing session without having my pages done. (Sometimes, I'd be up until 4 or 5 in the morning the night before to get them done, but, by golly, I got those darn pages written!) And so did Steve, my writing partner.

I slowly realize that the whole "go it alone to be a fully actualized human being" nonsense was, well, nonsense. I didn't have a word for it at the time, but Steve was my first real Accountability Partner.

When I started my online business several years ago, I flailed around a lot. An associate of mine was in a program where they were told to find an accountability partner. She called and asked me if I'd do it. Of course, I said, yes, partly because I already had a sense of how powerful it could be and partly because she was so far ahead of me in her own business and I knew I could benefit from any work I did with her. We had a form where we filled in stuff we'd get done that week, then email each other each evening with what we'd accomplished that day and what we promised to accomplish the next. We also talked regularly on the phone. Both of us got an amazing amount of stuff done, and both of our businesses flourished.

I was unwilling to write that nightly email and have to admit I hadn't accomplished everything I'd promised. Better to just get the stuff done.

It became obvious that I was getting a lot more benefit from the process than she did and we wound that down. (We still work together, of course, just not as accountability partners.) I tried finding another accountability partner and went through several. Each fizzled out for one reason or other. Then I was handed an accountability partner who I've now worked with for over a year and a half. We talk on the phone for a few moments every week day (baring a conflict in one of our schedules.) She lives on the East Coast and I'm on the West Coast, but we found a good time for both of us.

Each week, we make goals and promises for that week, write them down and email them to each other. Then, every day on the phone, we look at the promises we made the day before and make promises for the next day. It really works.

I highly recommend that everyone find an accountability partner. (Or a group; that can work, too.) You may go through several before finding the one that works. You may grow out of one after a long time and move on, but it's more than a valuable experience.

My partner and I have found a structure and rhythm that works well for us, but it is by no means the only way to do it. You can communicate by phone, by email, by text. You can even meet in person, if you live close by. You can do it every day, a few times a week, once a week. (Less than once a week doesn't seem very effective, but if it works for you, don't let me get in the way of that!)

You might write everything down, or be more fluid. You may use forms or take notes. (On our calls, I make a bullet point list of each of our promises every day and mail it to her. The next day we go over that list, then I make a new one.)

As you go forward, your structure will probably evolve. You may hear something someone else is doing that you like and add that to the mix. It's all guidelines, not rules, so don't get persnickety. (Or, if you're both persnickety, enjoy your mutual parsnicketyness! See? No rules.)

If you're in a group, you can have one "moderator" or trade off each time, or do free-for-all. You can give each one a specific amount of time for their turn, or let it flow organically. I tend to like more structure so things go smoothly and quickly, but that's me. I won't be on your call, so you don't have to worry about my curmudgeon-ness getting in your face.

When choosing an accountability partner, there are some things to look at:

- **Can you trust them?**
  You will be sharing things about yourself and your business, remember. I'm not recommending opening up the most secret corners of your darkest life and displaying them in all their shocking perfidy (in fact, I recommend you don't do that – it will muddy the water very quickly), but sometimes you will have to share something you're doing in your business that isn't yet ready for public consumption.

- **Are they responsible?**
  Sometimes, one or the other of you will fail to keep your promises. You are both human, it happens. If one person consistently doesn't keep promises, however, the other will feel no motivation to go the extra mile to keep theirs. This is good for neither of you.

- **Are they willing to hold you to your promises?**
  In a few of the groups I've been in, most of the time was spent justifying for each other why stuff didn't get done, and patting each other on the head, commiserating about how hard life was. This is worse than not productive or helpful. It's destructive.

- **Are you willing to hold them to theirs?**
  It has to be a two-way street. It should also, of course, be done with gentleness and kindness. At least that's my opinion. If you both like the Drill Sargent approach, have at each other! Again, I won't be there to stifle your boxing matches and some find a little blood sport really motivating. I prefer bunnies and puppies, but that's me.

- **Are you compatible?**
  You don't have to be in the exact same industry, but if one of you is in oil drilling and the other in Greenpeace, it probably won't work out well.

- **Do you like each other?**
  You don't have to become great friends, but you will be in contact often over a long period of time. Doing that with someone who simply rubs you the wrong way isn't going to help you be motivated to participate fully. And after working together for a long time, a true friendship may occur. That's a wonderful side benefit, but not necessary at all.

With most of these consideration, you won't really know until you've worked with them a while. Sometimes, things will become obvious right away. In either case, be willing to realize it's not working, communicate that kindly and simply and move on to someone else.

You are still ultimately responsible for your own life and your own accomplishments, of course. When your business or your life don't quite work out, it is not the fault or responsibility of your accountability partner or group. That part is up to you, entirely, so there is a little truth in all that "go it alone", rugged individual image we once all strived for. Yes, it is great to stand up on your own two feet, but when you have someone standing right next to you on theirs (and giving a hand if you occasionally wobble a bit), it makes life a whole lot nicer, don't you think? And when things don't work out, having someone you trust to make promises to while you pick yourself up, dust yourself off and indulge in other clichés will make the sting fade much more quickly.

Geoff Hoff is President and COO of Hunter's Moon Publishing, a company he created with Connie Ragen Green to help entrepreneurs write and publish books in order to enhance their credibility, grow their audience and be recognized as authorities in their field. He is a best-selling author and has been an actor, acting teacher, standup comic and popular blogger. He teaches courses in both creativity and in tech on the Internet.

Geoff grew up in a small town in Northern New Jersey that no longer exists, graduated from a small college in Spokane, Washington that no longer exists and has learned to distrust permanence.

You can find him at http://GeoffHoff.com When you visit his site, be sure to pick up his free report on what inspiration really is and how you can harness it for yourself and your business.

Chapter Ten

There is no Accountability without Authenticity
By Faydra Koenig

"Accountability is impossible without living an authentic life. All the best plans, action steps and brilliant ideas won't mean a thing if life isn't true. Inaction comes from knowing deep down that you aren't living in honor of yourself."

In 2013, I suffered a major setback in life that left me scared, alone and filled with shame. For almost an entire year, I found myself shrinking away from who I was in my truest sense. Once a vibrant, effervescent, larger-than-life personality, I found myself becoming emotionally atrophied and reclusive. In my depression, I lost the sense of who I was. I began living an inauthentic life, trying to convince myself that I wasn't suffering or that any suffering I was experiencing was necessary or evidence of my faith and willingness to bear a cross in the name of love. The result was a total loss of who I was as a person, total denial of my worth and constant heartache. In a matter of months, I lost significant contracts, friends and opportunities. It was such a horrible time, and because I was caught up in it and not the cause, I couldn't see any way out. I felt like a victim; I felt betrayed, and I was pretty mad at myself.

As a business owner, most of my outward life appeared to be going well. Being a type A personality helped me stay as focused as possible and many of the day-to-day activities were handled, but there was zero growth happening in my business. Living an inauthentic life had stolen my drive to expand, and I feared the worst from people, so I succumbed to inaction. For months, I talked the talk about business development. I even authored books that were amazing, but when it came time to promote myself, I stopped cold. I literally took no action towards any of the goals I claimed mattered so much to me. The pain of not living up to my potential was feeding into my depression and causing me to drift further into a mental abyss where there was no light, no happiness; all I could feel was the bottom of the pit.

Over time, I realized that I was suffering with situational depression and needed to find a way to process what I had been through. As a mental health professional, I knew that I was lost in a fog that could be lifted. I knew that deep down there were solutions if I would just allow myself to accept help. Knowing what we should do and taking action are two entirely different things. Sometimes in our weaknesses we fall into traps that perpetuate our suffering. It isn't that we welcome the dysfunction or desire to be drama-filled; on the contrary, life becomes so overwhelmingly big that our smallness seems unsurmountable and our self-imposed insignificance seems too real. It takes great courage and hope to believe that things can be restored and normalized again. If we are left without a sense of community and partnership there is no accountability to anyone other than ourselves, and a depressed person really doesn't hold their own feet to the fire.

In March of 2013, I attended a business women's retreat with the full intention of discussing my situation and seeking solutions to my problems. While convulsing physically and crying hysterically, I recounted how I had been caught up in a relationship with a man who had been accused of a crime prior to our marriage and how, though I believed in him and his innocence wholeheartedly, he was convicted and sent to prison for what amounts to the rest of his life. In a sacred circle of trust and confidentiality, I shared with total strangers the hate that had rained down on me since his conviction and how I, by default, had suffered tremendously even though I had absolutely nothing to do with anything he had been convicted of. In my pain and anguish, I shared how my reputation had suffered, how my relationships had been torn and how this imposed shame had left me emotionally bankrupt. I sat still after telling my story, waiting for the women in the group to shake their heads and tell me that they saw no way out for me and how sorry they felt for me. I waited for them to endorse the fact that the only real way out for me was either suicide or to live some form of reclusion, void of income or a meaningful existence in any form.

Amazingly, none of the women in the group reacted to me negatively. I had grown so accustomed to being rejected that it had become my default expectation. In the hours that followed my confession, I found that I began to feel lighter. I sensed an openness and easiness erupt from me like lava that had been held back by the Earth's crust. The intense pressure of my true nature could no longer be contained. In the space of acceptance and understanding, the "me" that had been suppressed for so long found its way out. The mask of quiet shame that I wore to appease the haters didn't fit in this environment. In this space, at the beach with other business women, I was able to be me...the real me, and it felt good. Over the course of the retreat, my true nature came back. I was laughing and joking and experiencing life authentically. I hadn't solved any of my problems, but I had allowed myself to be real and that, in and of itself, was a solution of sorts.

I left the women's retreat with a newfound desire to sift through the pain I was in. To find solutions that would render me eligible to be back in the game of life. I knew in my heart that I wasn't broken. I knew that the situation I was in didn't define me—I just didn't know how to break free. When we are lost in our own thoughts, we are slaves to the tapes that play in our heads, slaves to the trickster who lives inside that tells us we are a victim, life isn't fair and we are not worthy of what we want. The problem for me was that I was a seasoned professional who knew better, but didn't know how to take a step away from my situation and evaluate it on my own. In addition, I was now emotionally care-taking for a husband who was deteriorating psychologically, a widow without the death. I was dealing with the fall-out of the situation within the family and within the community and without any support for myself. The collapse of every hope and dream I had weighed heavily on me, and the only skill set I was using was denial. Denial kills our senses. It keeps us from living authentically because we don't agree with anything that is real. Denial can take many forms. For me, it looked like a constant convincing that I could do this. That I could manage the emotional shit storm that my spouse handed me on a near daily basis because, after all, I was home and he was gone. He had been the center of attention with his legal issues the entire time we had been together, and I had dutifully become the Proverbs wife, committed to long-suffering and selflessness in the name of "for richer, for poorer, in sickness and in health, in plenty and in want." The result: my inauthentic life began to crumble and my depression deepened.

In the spring of 2014, well after a year of being alone, I took an incredible step in the right direction. I got the solid help I needed to reclaim my authenticity. I allowed myself to believe that not only did I deserve to be free of the situation that I hadn't created, but had faced the full brunt of. I also deserved to regain all the ground I had lost and then some. I forgave myself for entering into a situation that ended badly and put to rest the part of me that questioned my own judgment. I came away from the situation authentically whole and that is when life took off again. To be clear, this realization took work. It took a leap of faith to love myself more than I loved someone else, which wasn't my default thought pattern. It took a willingness to face hard truths about myself and to get down to the bare bones of whether or not I wanted to be better and whether or not I wanted to honor myself. It would seem that the choice to love self over others should be easy. I can tell you it isn't. It requires bravery and accountability.

Accountability is impossible without living an authentic life. All the best plans, action steps and brilliant ideas won't mean a thing if life isn't true. Inaction comes from knowing deep down that you aren't living in honor of yourself. You can have the best business coaches, the most helpful support teams and none of it will cause you to take action if you are living in the shadows of who you know you are meant to be. By all accounts, my business should have been thriving. All the reviews of my books were positive and people loved my brand. I offered meaningful help. My issue was that I was so afraid of the unknowns and so disconnected from what I really wanted that I was sending mixed messages. The moment I admitted to myself how sad I really was, how disappointed I really was with how things had turned out and how much I really didn't want this life, everything changed. Until I was willing to own up to what I really wanted, I was stuck with nowhere to go but the bottom of the pit.

Since taking charge of my situation and by default, my life, things are changing rapidly. Of course they are not without setbacks, challenges and some uncertainty, but more importantly, I am not living in a double bind. I am no longer feeling wimpy and beaten down. I feel powerful and excited about life. I feel energized and eager to see what amazing thing is going to happen next. By living authentically, the action steps I need to take in business are clear, and I am motivated to do whatever it takes to complete them. I no longer sit and think, "I know what I need to do, but there are a million reasons why I can't, shouldn't or won't." I am not allowing a situation completely out of my control to define me or my business. I am standing up for myself and in agreement with what I always knew to be true—I am a wonderful woman who has a ton of benefit to add to the world.

Since owning my story and letting go of what isn't my story, everything about life is changing. My demeanor and my motivations are different and that results in better and more fulfilling relationships. I am in a community with men and women who know who I am and what I am managing, and they are determined to 'see me succeed. They are accountability partners who are in a relationship with me under totally transparent circumstances, and that feels amazing. My authenticity invites them to support me and to call me out if they see me backslide.

If I were to offer advice to anyone about accountability, it wouldn't be based on the nuts-and-bolts tactics to take action steps. When you have overcome something traumatic, you look at life differently. Procrastination or fear of success or whatever puny excuses people use to avoid action make me laugh. Those are symptoms of something much bigger. My advice wouldn't be to tackle the practical side of accountability. My advice would be to get honest about how authentically you are living your life. Be real. When you take ownership of your life, when you grab the issues in your life by the balls and squeeze really hard and say, "Submit to my will," something wonderful happens. Any action you need to take becomes effortless. Any consequences you must face feel worth the risk and any glorious outcomes are yours for the taking.

Faydra Koenig, MA is a mental health professional, author, speaker, podcaster and certified life coach. She works with men and women to help them avoid the pitfalls of divorce and get the lives they deserve. You can find Faydra's podcast, Coming Out Of The Fire, on iTunes. Find her on the web at http://www.americasdivorcecoach.us and look for her books on Amazon. She is a weekly newspaper columnist for her hometown newspaper, the Red Bluff Daily News where she inspires her audience to make lasting changes in their lives.

Chapter Eleven

Accountability Partnerships Through The Years
By Felicia J. Slattery, M.A., M.Ad.Ed.

> *"We each knew the guidelines of what we were supposed to do and all three of us were excited about the program. So we dove in, honoring our weekly appointment, helping each other create goals, and moving forward through the content together as a cohesive unit."*

The year I first began my business in 2006, I was fortunate enough to be "forced" into an accountability situation. Now, normally you don't see the words "fortunate" and "forced" together in the same sentence, but that's exactly what happened. Here's the story:

As an academic, I had spent years teaching students how to write and deliver speeches, as well as how to develop effective communication skills for business and personal relationships. That much I knew very well. What I didn't know was how to run a business, least of all run a business from my home. So I signed up for a comprehensive online course, which, as far as I knew when I signed up was mostly based on a live teleseminar training component (my favorite way to learn!). During the first teleseminar of the class, while listening to the instructor lay down the rules and expectations of the 12-week program, I realized there was one important component of the program the most successful students took full advantage of in the past: being active and accountable to two "buddy coaches."

While working through the program, we were assigned to spend one hour each week via phone with two other classmates on the call. We were to break the hour into three equal parts and each spend 20 minutes being "buddy coached" by our peers from the class. I remember immediately thinking, "That is silly. I don't know who I'm going to end up with. I just want the class training; I don't need to talk to those other people." However, with a master's degree in adult education and training, as well as having been a teacher myself, I know instructors don't just add significant pieces like that to a curriculum without a solid reason. So there I was being forced to be in this buddy coaching situation with two strangers. Sigh.

Before getting on the first call, I reminded myself of one of the life lessons I taught my daughters, which I also share with my audiences when I speak: life is more fun when you play along. So rather than grudgingly going into the first buddy call, staring at the clock, putting in my time simply waiting for it to be over, I eagerly joined in, throwing myself into the unknown process, ready to allow whatever was going to unfold. And I'm so glad I did because it was like magic.

We each knew the guidelines of what we were supposed to do and all three of us were excited about the program. So we dove in, honoring our weekly appointment, helping each other create goals, and moving forward through the content together as a cohesive unit.

After the 12 weeks of the program had ended, we weren't quite ready to say goodbye to our weekly meetings. We'd built a good rapport and could see positive changes. Plus, I'll admit, in those early days of my business, I was lonely working at home by myself in between my daughters' nap schedules (at the time they were two and four years old,) and I didn't have anyone in my life I could speak to about building the kind of business I wanted. So instead of disbanding at the end of the required time, we continued meeting weekly for about a year. Around that time, one of our members got busy with work and life and decided to stop meeting. However, two of us couldn't bear to see it all end. We had each received so much value from the other, so much help, and pushed each other forward to success after success, we knew the only way to make that continue was to remain together regularly meeting for what had become an accountability call as much as it was buddy coaching.

Although through the years the final two of us have stopped and restarted a few times due to various work, family, and health issues, my very first buddy coach and I are still working together to this very day. In fact as I write these words, just yesterday we were on the phone and I was helping her to "talk" her book and she was coaching me through an issue that is her area of expertise. It's been fun to be with her as we each have grown our businesses from literally nothing but an idea to achieving some cool things like:

- Six completed books written and published between us; as well as contributed chapters to dozens of other books. More than one of those books became #1 Amazon category best-sellers.
- Dozens of online products created, launched, and made profitable.
- Built countless profitable websites, sales pages, squeeze pages, and more.
- Wrote hundreds of articles, recorded dozens of videos, and posted to blogs since 2006.
- We've made hundreds of thousands of dollars doing work that we love and that enriches our lives as well as the lives of those we serve.
- She's married the man of her dreams (one of her goals when we started working together) and I improved my marriage beyond what I could have imagined was possible.
- And hundreds of little accomplishments all along the way, both personal and professional, that might have seemed small in the moment, but by building step-by-step as we continue to meet regularly, over time we repeatedly see the little accomplishments add up to the big giant goals we've each wanted to achieve.

As a result of that wonderful relationship and positive experience, I have actively sought out more accountability partners over the years, having as many as four at one time. I'm now down to two regular accountability partners and I work with them each on different aspects of my life and business (and yes, one is my original buddy coach!).

Here are a few lessons I've learned about working effectively with an accountability partner that might help you, too.

- The relationship works best when you come together as equals and treat each other as such.
- Choose a person you either already have a great relationship with or someone who you meet as you are working on a specific program, course, or goal together.
- The more often you meet, and the more regularly you meet, the more you each get done. (This seems counterintuitive, because it feels like you might be taking an hour per week away from your productivity, but having that person you know you'll have to speak to in just a few days pushes you to get things you promised done!)
- Be willing to help with extra things outside your regularly scheduled meeting times. Occasionally something will come up that one or the other of you will need a quicker answer on, such as an opinion on a sales page or a new graphic or longer help with, like recording thoughts for a book.
- Establish some ground rules and expectations. When everyone knows the rules it's so much easier to play nicely together and avoid feelings getting hurt. See the next section for what some of those rules might be.

After reading this book, you'll have some fantastic ideas about working with an accountability partner. Some of the other authors may have their own lists to share. Based on my experiences, here are some questions you may want to consider as you embark on setting up your accountability partnership so you can avoid potential pitfalls and miscommunication:

Meeting Considerations:
- How often will you meet? Will it be on a regular schedule or change from week to week depending on

your calendars? (I will add here a regular appointment that you plan other things around actually works best!)

- How will you divide the time when you meet? And how will you manage it? Will you use a timer stopping and switching to the other person when it goes off, simply allow the conversation to flow naturally, or something in between?
- Who will start and will it be the same every time or will you switch back and forth?
- Will you come to the meeting having completed some sort of written update via email or form/questionnaire or will the updating and accountability piece be spoken?
- How will you handle cancellations both at the last minute when a minor (or major) emergency shows up and/or when you know in advance you'll be unavailable?
- Will you take breaks for the holidays, summer vacation, or some other built-in times off from your meetings?
- Will you meet in person, via phone, via Skype or Google Hang-Out video, smoke signals, or some other way?

Money Considerations:
- Will you be giving each other access to all of your products and services, providing a family/friends discount, or want each other to pay full price? There are arguments to each of these. Either way, decide consciously, not by accident.
- If one or both of you has an affiliate program, and it makes sense to promote each other, either to your community of subscribers or your social media communities, will you be paying an affiliate commission to each other or not? Likewise, if you

have a referral program, will you pay your typical referral fee when the situation arises?

- When you need each other to help beyond your regular meeting times, will that be on a paid or free basis?
- What does "taking advantage" of the other person look like to you and what does feeling like you're being taken advantage of look like to you?

Between Meetings:
- What will happen between meetings when you have a quick something or other to share or help with? What is your preferred method of contact? Email? Text? Phone call at work number, home number, or private cell? Private message on a social media site you both frequent? Skype or other text chat?
- What will be the expected response time for in between meeting contact? Is it within 3 hours? 24 hours? 3 days? Only during work times?

Overall:
- How long do you plan to continue in the accountability relationship? Will it be indefinite or associated with a particular program, course or goal and end when the program or course ends or when the goal is achieved?
- At what point will you pause to consciously and systematically assess how things are going?
- What criteria will you use to determine if you will continue moving forward or stop meeting?
- How will you know for sure if the accountability is giving you what you need? How will you measure the success both together and individually?
- If your accountability partner is in a business where you are connected with someone else who could be considered a "competitor" to her or him, what

protocol will you establish on promoting the other person and their products and/or services? (For example, I would be crushed if any of my accountability partners suddenly started promoting another speech coach offering the same kinds of things I offer, but would have no problem if they were to actively promote another professional speaker. They know this, so we're all good.)

- Do you expect each other to be exclusive in your accountability relationship or will you "date around" and have more than one accountability partner, perhaps for different aspects of your life?

You may not have the answers to all these pieces up front. In fact, I almost never have. And on several occasions I had to clarify many of these issues. Some you don't have to agree on out loud up front and others you should include as part of your conversation around deciding to work with someone or not.

You see, there is an interpersonal communication principle that says we assume people are like us. However, the reality is, there is not one human being on the planet who thinks 100% like us in 100% of all situations. Therefore, planning ahead and consciously creating the relationships you want, whether with an accountability partner or anyone else, means being aware of and open to discussing each other's expectations. When you can do that, you're on your way to achieving a remarkable, and possibly life-changing professional relationship that can easily allow everyone involved, and those you touch because of it, to flourish.

Felicia J. Slattery, M.A., M.Ad.Ed., is on a mission to motivate, inspire and train smart business owners and entrepreneurs to create meaningful connections through effective communication and public speaking. An internationally-acclaimed, award-winning speaker, best-selling author, and the creator of the trademarked Signature Speech™ system, Felicia presents to audiences large and small on topics related to communication, speaking, and being a successful entrepreneur in spite of everything life can throw at you. As a cancer survivor, Felicia's enthusiastic passion for communication is contagious because she knows that one important message delivered with power can transform a life. She works with experts and entrepreneurs, as well as CEOs and celebrities to help them more effectively communicate their messages on and off stages while building and maintaining strong relationships locally, nationally, and globally, both in person and virtually using the Internet. You can find out more about Felicia at http://FeliciaSlattery.com .

Chapter Twelve

Accountability in the New Economy
By Meredith Eisenberg

"When you transition to working for yourself the game changes. You are no longer "held accountable" - nobody cares when you work, or if you are dressed."

"The only way to do great work is to love what you do"
-Steve Jobs

We are going through a Revolution - bigger than the Industrial Revolution. Technology is quickly sorting us out into "owner" and "workers". Owners have the ability to control the technology - to enjoy freedom that wasn't possible before the Internet. Workers will get paid less and less and will have their every step increasingly dictated by the computer. There is no love in being a worker.

My mission, as founder of the Launch Ladies, is to help people end up on the right side of the new economy. I teach people step by step how to make a decent living sharing their passion with others.

It's a mission I believe in with my whole heart - but it's not easy. According to the Wall Street Journal, over 75% of start up businesses fail in the first 5 years. I've been in business now for over 7 years - and work with clients who have been sharing their brilliance online for over 10 years. I also have worked with many clients who spun their wheels, worked very hard, yet ended up having to give up the business and get a job.

Both groups of clients were very smart and very talented. They both had amazing gifts to offer and a solid market of ideal clients to serve. So, what separates the successful businesses from the failures?

I've thought about it a lot. It all boils down to accountability. Moving from work in an office to work for yourself is a huge transition. In an office, there are people there to keep you accountable. You are expected to come into the office at a certain time, to copy people on memos, to write reports of your results. All of this creates a built-in sense of accountability. You don't want to let your co-workers down, and you may be thinking you are lucky to have any kind of job when so many don't, so you work hard.

When you transition to working for yourself the game changes. You are no longer "held accountable" - nobody cares when you work, or if you are dressed. There are no reports to fill out (especially if you don't have any clients yet). You sit in front of your computer screen, free at last, untethered. The problem is that without the tether of someone to report to, it is very unlikely that you'll get the work done. Unfortunately, for many of us, it is hard to let other people down, but very easy to not keep promises to ourselves. (If you've ever started to try to lose weight by yourself and failed - you know exactly what I'm talking about).

I've noticed that the clients who end up building successful and growing businesses have set up accountability systems for themselves. There are as many different ways of setting up accountability as there are business owners. Here are a few different ways I've added accountability to my business.

Take a class I started my online marketing business as a virtual assistant. To get started, I took a class offered by AssistU which teaches people how to set up a virtual assistant business, how to interview clients, how to set up your legal framework, how to price your services, etc. We had to turn in homework assignments weekly that gently guided us through the whole process. The other students in the class provided excellent motivation to get everything done.

Hire a coach If you've moved past the "setting up the basics", hiring a coach is an essential move. All of my successful clients have business coaches - even the business coaches have business coaches - and it's no coincidence. A good coach will hold your feet to the fire - and remind you of your promises. Just know that they can't "make" you do anything - but the fact that you've spent a lot of money, and have promised your mentor a result - will go a long way toward ensuring that you get it done. My coach has been instrumental in keeping me to my word and helping me to develop a passion based business.

Join a mastermind group I joined a mastermind group that gave points for achieving your goals each week. Because I didn't want to let my fellow mastermind participants down - I've stayed up to all hours of the night finishing projects. In some ways, mastermind groups are even more powerful than individual coaching because there are more people involved. The combination that has worked well for me is a coach plus a mastermind group. The coach gives strategy ideas and the mastermind makes sure that I get them done.

Create a partnership My business began to take off as soon as I partnered with my current co-founder. Not only is it good to have someone to bounce ideas off, you work harder because somebody else is depending on you.

Hire an assistant When I was a virtual assistant, my clients would often say that although I did very high quality work - the value I brought was simply having someone else invested in the success of their business. A good assistant can help "manage" you, remind you of your goals and nag you to make sure that you get them done.

Use your social networks Let your networks know what you are up to. If you want to write a book, post that on Facebook. Or, even better, send a message out to your list asking for help writing the book. This works even for small things. Just today, I accidentally posted a workout I created in a fitness program on Facebook. The fact that 6 people I care about liked the Facebook post - made me finish the workout. I felt like I had made a promise.

Try a coworking space. Is is hard to get work done when you are home alone? Do you miss talking with co-workers? Is working out of the local coffee shop getting you too addicted to $7 lattes? You might want to try a coworking space. Coworking spaces are cooperative/collaborative office spaces where virtual workers work together in the same physical space. I've been a member of my co-working space for 2 years and it has made a tremendous difference. Not only do I get more work done, I found 3 team members from my co-workers (and they all keep me very accountable).

These are just a few ways to create accountability in your business. The most successful business owners I know use multiple accountability methods to keep themselves focused and on track.

The thread that ties these 7 tips together is that they all involve other people. I think the biggest mistake solo business owners make is trying to work by themselves. Human beings are social creatures - they are designed to work with others - and it is very difficult to create a thriving business without any feedback or support.

It is important to remember though - creating all the accountability in the world won't help you if you aren't holding yourself accountable for the right things. Steven Covey talks about being careful when setting your goals - so that your ladder is on the right wall. Accountability works the same way - you need to make sure that the steps you are taking are actually going to lead you to your goal.

Working with other people, in addition to helping you get things done, can provide valuable feedback in terms of whether you are doing the right things. This is especially important for solopreneurs - even if you don't have an "official" staff - you can create a team of coaches, assistants and mastermind partners to test your ideas and strategies and make sure that the steps you are taking are actually in line with your goals.

So, where do you want to land in the new economy? Do you want the freedom to use technology to make a living on your own terms? Or would you like to be a worker - held accountable by technology? If you would like to make a living on your own terms, one of the essential elements to creating a thriving business is to build an accountability support network into your business. What are you waiting for? Pick up the phone, call a few friends - offer to support each other. And... start building something amazing.

Meredith Eisenberg has a passion for helping solopreneurs to make a living on their own terms by teaching and sharing their passions with others.

As founder of the Launch Ladies, Meredith can cut through all the "technology fog" and help you create a thriving business based on your skills and brilliance.

Meredith draws upon her 7 years of online marketing experience in the coaching world, and 15 years of marketing and PR experience creating award winning campaigns for local governments to help her clients build the systems and strategies needed to create a thriving business.

Need help choosing the right tools for your business? Go to http://thelaunchladies.com and pick up your free video, checklist and e-book on choosing the right e-mail and e-commerce tools for your business.

Chapter Thirteen

Accountability "HACKS" to Get Motivated
By Adam Urbanski

> *"If you are not disciplined, then your entire life is driven by fear, you will always need an external push. It is good to have a little bit of that push, but without a good dose of self-discipline, it will be hard to accomplish much."*

Today I am called the Millionaire Marketing Mentor ® by people around the world but bottom line is I was truly blessed early on to have people who held me accountable to actually make progress and grow both as a person and as an entrepreneur.

When I came to the United States I didn't have much. I came with $194 and was able to turn that into a very successful business in the restaurant industry and now into another business in the coaching, consulting, information marketing and sold millions of dollars of coaching, consulting services and information products .

I think that if I were left to my own devices early on, when I was so much younger, I would have not gotten to where I am, I would not have had enough of the tools and internal motivation. Thankfully, I had other people around to motivate me, to push me and to cheer me on. At first it was such a simple thing as having a boss at a job. Later, it was having partners in business who knew better or knew more. This way I had a proverbial "axe" hanging over my head and things had to be done.

In our business today, we provide a little bit of similar accountability for other people so that they can grow their companies faster. We assist entrepreneurs at three different stages of business growth. For those who are at the starting point, we help them take their ideas and quickly turn them into profitable businesses. Then there are entrepreneurs who have businesses, have things to sell, or services to offer. Self-employed people typically don't know how to attract clients so we help them find ways to turn what they do into a system to attract and retain clients. And finally, for those who have successful companies, we help them maximize and leverage hidden revenue/profit centers. We show them how to exploit things that already exist in their business, but are overlooked.

Once we help them realize what those hidden opportunities are, their businesses can be more successful.

Everybody has a personal relationship with accountability. Our perspective and opinion on what it is changes. Very few people have this innate drive to accomplish; it has to be instilled to begin with. If we, for example, let kids just be, they will likely become a bunch of uneducated and lazy bums. They will go with the flow, with what's easy. If you don't hold kids accountable for grades on tests, to graduate from class to class, then what's the point of doing anything. There's no reward, no punishment, no external accountability.

External accountability, especially with regards to entrepreneurs, is a double edged sword. We typically exit the corporate world and whatever career we're in – corporate or academic –to not be accountable to someone else any longer. In that world somewhere, somehow we had someone else telling us what to do and asking us to report back to get things done or we would be fired or penalized. We hated having that answerability! Becoming an entrepreneur is like the proverbial "sticking it to the man". We don't want to be working for the man anymore, so we go and strike out on our own.

But then guess what happens? Now we crave this accountability because, left to our own devices, we're typically lost. There are so many opportunities to explore, so many avenues to pursue that it becomes impossible to decide. We need some kind of external pressure! We miss it.

The way I see it there are different kinds accountability – external and internal. External one is having a boss, supervisor, friend, someone who is telling us what to do and if we don't do it we won't get promoted, we won't get that raise and we might get fired. That's actually a pretty shabby sort of motivation, by pain and fear. On the other hand, there's an internal drive, this true motivation - it is your WHY, what you are going after, your DREAM. If the dream is big enough, you'll start finding where to hold yourself accountable to do what needs to be done.   And that accountability ultimately translates for me into DISCIPLINE.

If you are not disciplined, then your entire life is driven by fear, you will always need an external push. It is good to have a little bit of that push, but without a good dose of self-discipline, it will be hard to accomplish much.

There's this movie "City Slackers" in which the character Curly, this rough cowboy, dies with his finger pointing out to the sky saying "you've got to go to figure this one thing out". And I have a friend who kept telling me: "we are all destined for greatness, the only thing that holds you back is you have to discover THAT ONE THING!" Nobody knows what that one thing is, that's the lifelong pursuit and it changes for people.

Our life's mission is to discover what that one thing is. And then, after finding it, to fulfil it. That's what brings us happiness. This one thing is our intrinsic motivation. If we don't have it, we wander in the dark. Sometimes we stumble upon a room that has light turned on, and sometimes we're totally clueless. That's when procrastination kicks in, that's when we need a lot of external help to push us and to cheer us on.

I personally believe that as human creatures we are inherently lazy. We'll find all sorts of ways to do nothing or do the least possible that needs to be done unless it is something we are excited about, and this only until our enthusiasm wears off. So we have to find ways to keep us going, to hold ourselves motivated.

There are two things to keep us on course. First one is SYSTEMS. Systems are nothing more than routines or habits. Habits can be good or bad. If you develop bad habits, you don't need much accountability. You will be doing things you've always done, always the same way. If you develop good habits, they are routine behaviors, you don't need reminders, you do them naturally. You are fine as long as you keep doing them regularly. Just like brushing your teeth daily!

The second thing to keep ourselves responsible is what I call HACKS. These are also routines but a bit more sporadic. It is something that you do occasionally, a shortcut, a trick you employ so that you get done what needs to get done.

For me, the daily habit is avoiding turning on email first thing in the morning so I don't get swept away solving someone else's problems. Another habit is journaling. It's an example of internal self-accountability. And I don't mean entries like "Dear diary, today I broke my nail". It is more of self- reflection – what have I accomplished, and what I haven't accomplished, what did I say to myself, what got in the way, what excuses did I use, how did I allow myself to let this get in my way, and what more am I willing to do … We really have this amazing ability to sense our own BS. We know when we are lying to ourselves. Journaling can go either way. We can let ourselves off the hook easily, just like we lie to other people, but inside our heads we know that we are making up a story.

Journaling is an example of being accountable to the toughest boss or a dearest friend to whom you'll never lie, or if you are religious, like going to confession... If you treat journaling that way, it can be an incredible accountability tool. So in an essence you answer to yourself. That's where it starts for me. If you are looking for someone else to hold you responsible, then you are reacting and not taking action in your life.

Great example of occasional hacks for me is scheduling public deadlines. I will schedule something and announce it publicly so that I have to do it. I remember the time when we were running a live event and we were giving people handouts still hot of the printer. Attendees didn't pay attention but the truth is that they were created just a few minutes before. I was procrastinating and I was so much in my head. Sometimes we do that in business, not because we're lazy but because there's so much going on and we have so many different thoughts, so unless there's this hard deadline, it is like this mission impossible.

For me using public accountability and setting public deadlines is a huge motivator. I remember a few years ago signing up for Spartan Race a year in advance with my nephew and friend. I was on top of my shape but things got in the way and I did not work out as much as I should. Then the time came to run the race. And two things worked for me. I had enough of the internal motivation to just go and do it to have a satisfaction of finishing and not being the last one, and the second thing, there was at least another person ready to do it with me. So there was this external accountability, not to let someone else down.

Another hack is surrounding yourself with people you want to be accountable to. Big companies have boards of directors, publically traded companies have shareholders, they have to report results so it has huge impact and consequences. As a small company, solopreneurs, we usually don't have that. If we mess up, we eat mac and cheese for a month; if we do great, we take a vacation. There's no one you have to answer to. The way to hack it is to surround yourself with two, three, five people you answer to. Make a commitment to them that once a month or once a quarter you will let them know where you are in your business.

The simplest way to have this kind of accountability is Mastermind. I have a friend with whom I have been checking in on a regular basis for years. Sometimes I don't know if I want to hang up on her or thank her! She is holding me accountable and telling me what I NEED to hear not what I WANT to hear. And it can be tough. But we need this push to accomplish things. So in my personal Mastermind, just before meeting, it means staying up all night, knowing that I have to show up with things I promised I would do and having them completed.

Another example is teaming up with another person who can be our accountability buddy or success mate. Sometimes it's the easiest to give up on ourselves. But when we are responsible to someone else, we will frequently do more, knowing that their success is attached ours. We will go further and we will work harder just to not let the other person down.

The biggest point is that there is no external accountability without internal drive. People who live only by outside motivation live miserable lives. They constantly feel pushed, unrewarded, threatened, they live the life of victimhood. They don't have internal mechanisms to get ahead. That internal mechanism is clarity on what really matters and making it so important that you will do whatever it takes, however long it takes to reach it.

Another hack for being accountable is also finding tricks to put yourself in situations that will motivate you to do more. A few years ago, we ran a little contest for our clients where they had 2-3 days to create something new in their business and make as much money with it as they could. And people made anywhere from $6,000 - $8,000 all the way to $18,000 over the weekend. The motivating part was (a) I want to win (b) I want to show up strong (c) I don't want to be a loser or look stupid and (d) if I do well I make more money. So the situation itself creates accountability.

When you create this "public accountability" for yourself, three things are needed. First COURAGE, because by putting yourself on a line and stating that by such and such day you will have so and so accomplished, it takes some resolution, some grit. Second, it requires FAITH in your own ability to pull that off. Because if you hesitate even for a moment, it's like you lost. Without that you will let other things get in the way instead of doing what needs to be done. The third thing is CONFIDENCE. If you did what needs to be done and you feel good about it, your internal self-worth keeps growing and you get bigger and bolder. But if you don't reach your goals and you give up on yourself, it erodes your self-confidence. That's when you need external "cheerleaders".

At any given time in life and business we need different types of support. We need someone who pushes us and cheerleaders who, regardless of our accomplishments, help us keep this confidence in ourselves. They tell us to keep going when we are at our lowest.

People are motivated by different things. Men for example are motivated by results. When they do well, they feel good. Women on the other hand, when they feel good, they accomplish more. For women an intrinsic sense of motivation is even more powerful. They need a bigger vision to rally around. Men are fired up initially by just getting things done and instant rewards like making money, driving fancy cars and so on. Men see, do, think and constantly need to get validated. Then they look for more altruistic goals to transform the world. Women want validation upfront, they want a more communal vision, they want to change the world, and make sure that everyone is fine before they take any action. So the initial triggers are quite different.

We don't need accountability to do things we've always done. We have certain routines, we don't need much motivation. The point is, things that we've always done have gotten us exactly where we are. So where accountability comes into place is when we need to do something differently, something that we haven't accomplished before.

A perfect example is a child wanting to walk. Imagine how huge her/his internal inspiration is. There is really not much external motivation. There is a big drive, despite all the stumbles and falls to do it. What happens gradually in life is this natural, innate drive you had as a kid changes and you need three things to get going.

First of all you need to know your WHY, you have to have your compelling reason, this ONE THING. Secondly, you have to have a CONTEXT or supportive environment. And the last one is what I call TRIGGER mechanisms. Triggers are usually some traumatic events, dramatic changes, turning points like school reunion, milestone birthdays etc. They either "happen" or you have to figure those out for yourself. For example – a couple of years ago I did get into exercising using P90X method. My WHY - I wanted to lose some weight, I wanted to live a healthier life. Supportive environment – it was simple to use a CD and exercise along with the instructor on the TV screen. My trigger – I was turning 40, going on a cruise with my clients and wanted to look and feel good. So the magic to keeping yourself motivated is having the reason, the support structure and creating your own triggers.

One final advice I have is to regularly take time to immerse yourself in "nothingness". What I mean is to be reflective, just stop and be with yourself, with your thoughts. For me being from Poland and having had hard-working parents with solid work ethics, it is the toughest thing to do. I have thoughts that stopping and doing nothing is being lazy and not productive. The thing is that if you are constantly on the go, you eventually end up not being efficient at all. So it's a great idea to regularly take time, stop doing, in a physical sense, and think. Henry Ford says "thinking is one of the hardest things that people do" and so few do it. Think in terms of what you want to achieve, how you want your life and business to be, and how you want to get there. This kind of thinking is hard, it is scary, it requires courage, faith and confidence.

Nowadays, with everything that we have access to, life is too short not to do what you want to do. So do what you are passionate about and as Gary Vaynerchuk says "Crush it"! We need to find out our biggest why, that "one thing" that drives us. Maryanne Williamson tells us "'Who am I to be brilliant, gorgeous, talented, fabulous?' Actually, who are you not to be?" Be THAT, find your WHY and go for it! Surround yourself with people who support you and buy into your dream, who encourage you to do better than your best and cheer you when you think you don't have anything left in you. And remember that ultimately you are not accountable to anyone else but you!

Adam Urbanski, founder of TheMarketingMentors.com, is a secret weapon behind some of today's biggest entrepreneurial success stories. Tens of thousands of coaches, consultants and other entrepreneurial professionals use his no-nonsense, easy to implement marketing strategies to turn ideas into successful businesses that make a big impact and generate profits fast!

Chapter Fourteen

Using Accountability to Help Set Boundaries
By Kristen Eckstein

> *"This is an example of exactly what the word "accountability" means to me. ... It's having someone in my corner who I know will look me in the eye and in a firm, loving voice say, "STOP IT" when I start down a path of self-destruction."*

Today I was sitting across my local banker inquiring about a car loan to purchase the car I'd been leasing for the past few years. As he looked up my information and my business name that my car is registered under—Imagine Studios, LLC—he asked the next logical question, "What do you do?" And I answered with my usual 10-second description, "I start publishing companies for entrepreneurs."

He stopped writing, looked up at me and said, "Wow! I've been in business a long time and *never* met anyone who has such a cool job!" In that moment I wondered why last week I felt like throwing in the towel and running away from it all to go work across the street at our local Hobby Lobby. What I do *is* really cool. I get to work with other driven entrepreneurs—people who "get" me because they're just as crazy as I am—and help them make their dreams come true and exponentially grow their businesses.

When I let that sink in, I sit back and have the same reaction my banker had, "Wow!"

As I mentioned, just a week ago I felt like giving it all up and going to get a run-of-the-mill day job working for "the man." And when I felt like that, I immediately went to my business coach and told her I'd about had it. I'd had it with the hours, I was tired, cranky, and sick of letting everyone in the world think I don't sleep so I'm available 24/7. And she took 10 minutes out of her day to tell me, "Stop it." I'd been beating myself up for not being the superhero of the business world, and she reminded me, "Even ninjas need their rest. Don't let these people and situations have power over you."

This is an example of exactly what the word "accountability" means to me. It's not just someone reminding me of my goals and helping me when I get stuck. It's not just hiring a business coach, life coach, speaking coach, etc. (of which I have all three). It's having someone in my corner who

I know will look me in the eye and in a firm, loving voice say, "STOP IT" when I start down a path of self-destruction.

This style of accountability has kept me from completely giving up. It's helped me be there for my clients when they need me most, and not allow them to own me. It's made me take *time* to recharge, to rest, and to give myself permission to ignore email for an hour or two. The fact coaches continue to remind me of is that most people may think it's an emergency, but if I'm not taking care of *me* first, it *will* become an emergency when I screw something up with their books.

In addition to accountability to take time for myself and my accountability to a coach to grow my business and get that next project done, I'm a member of two other forms of accountability: a group and a dear friend.

My accountability group meeting consists of about six members that meet via the GoToWebinar system twice a month. We each give an update as to what we accomplished since the last meeting and how we made money with what we did, or how we plan to make money with it in the coming weeks. We also ask for help on any areas where we're stuck and feedback on our ideas. It's a combination of an accountability group with a tiny bit of masterminding sprinkled in, and it's been working very well for me to help me set goals and stay on task with how those goals directly impact my bottom line.

My close friend and I meet once a week on video via Skype and update each other on our personal lives and businesses. We support each other and hold each other accountable to invest in outside support when needed (like a business coach), and since we're both women with husbands who work with us, we have an entirely different issue to deal with—men who want to solve all our problems when all we want to do is vent about a few frustrations. Our support structure runs deeper than a simple accountability check-in, as we brainstorm ideas and perspectives, keep each other from overcomplicating our projects, and coach each other to success. It's a fun blend of catching up with a friend, accountability, and brainstorming.

As a result of my personal success using these various systems for holding myself accountable in my business and personal life, I decided to start a mastermind group for aspiring and published authors who need support and accountability to get their books written, published, and successfully marketed. *My Book Mastermind* started as a training program, and my members quickly let me know that's not what they wanted. What they want—and are willing to pay for—is ongoing accountability to their goals and learner-directed training in the form of coaching and Q&A calls. This is actually easier for me to deliver than the trainings I had been putting together for them, so in May of 2014 I re-launched the program with a focus in these three main areas:

- **Goal Setting**—Every Monday I post a "Monday Goal Post" in the Facebook group and have everyone who wants to post what their goals are for that week. They *love* this activity as they've actually seen progress by writing their goals down and knowing other people are reading them!
- **Accountability**—Every Friday I post a "Friday Check-In" in the Facebook group where everyone checks in with an update to their previous Monday goals. I also give them an extra nudge and ask what they're planning to do over the weekend to complete their weekly goal and prepare for the next week's goal.
- **Group Coaching**—Inevitably, my members will get "stuck" and need some outside guidance. So I implemented two live calls each month. One is a group coaching Q&A call where they can ask any question and I answer as many as I can during the 45 minutes. The other is a 30-minute Fishbowl Hotseat session where one "lucky" (that term has yet to be set in

stone) member gets one-on-one coaching with me and the others get to watch and listen.

The reason I chose these three areas is quite literally because I asked them what they wanted and this is what they came back with. It made me step back and realize just how *important* a structured system of accountability is, how much it's needed, and that people actually *do* want someone to not just hold their hand through a process, but kick their "buts" into gear to accomplish their goals. ("But" being the excuses that hold us back from making progress.) Now it's obvious to me how necessary a reliable accountability system is to our success as entrepreneurs, and what it takes to create a healthy accountability system that actually works.

Not every system works. I've had many coaches over the years, and the ones that have helped me the most are the ones that check in regularly with me and ask me how I'm coming on my goals. In my karate academy, goal setting is the life skill focus four months out of each year. They stress goal setting in every class, the instructors ask students to give them an update on how they're doing in school and at home, in addition to how they're doing focusing on their karate skills, and they have multiple reward systems in place to help students name, track, and stay accountable to reaching their personal and martial arts goals.

With all my experience in the wide world of accountability and all the shapes and forms it can take, I've never seen an instance when it wasn't a necessary part of someone's success. If you're not accountable to anyone except yourself, I urge you to change that as soon as possible. Here are some ways you can find people to help you stay accountable to your goals:

- **Hire a Coach**—A good coach (life, business, etc.) will help you clarify your goals, set achievable goals, and hold you accountable to reach them. You may have to go through a few coaches before you find one you really "click" with, and if you have a good coach, that coach will know when you're ready to graduate on to someone else. A good coach doesn't want you to stay with them forever. They want you to outgrow what they can do for you and watch you soar!

- **Find a Friend**—My friend approached me because we'd mostly lost touch over the past few years and she wanted time to catch up with me. Now we not only spend time "catching up," but we hold each other accountable for results in our businesses, and even partner on projects.
- **Form a Group**—There is no rule that states you can't get a group of friends or business buddies together and start meeting bi-weekly, weekly, or even just once a month. The group I'm in began with one person inviting a select group of others to join his inner circle. It's a blend of people with different backgrounds, interests, and styles of business. In fact, about the only thing we have in common is our love for the event that brought us all together and the fact we're all entrepreneurs! If you form your own group, look for people who are not in your niche and are at different levels in their businesses from each other. That melting pot of ideas and backgrounds is what will keep your group exciting and engaging.

I hope I've been able to impart a spark of ideas for how you can find someone or a group of someones to hold you accountable to set, reach, and move beyond your goals. I've had some form of accountability since I first started my business, and it's by far one of the *best* decisions I ever made that directly impacted my success!

Kristen Eckstein is a highly sought-after publishing authority, multi best-selling author and award winning international speaker who has started over 50 publishing companies and published over 170 books and e-books. In Fall 2013 she challenged herself to write and published a new Kindle book every week for 18 weeks straight, and in 2014 she started the Kindle in 30 Challenge, the Kindle to Print Challenge, and the My Book Mastermind programs to help aspiring authors set, reach, and achieve their goals for authorpreneurial success. In "real life," she's studying for her black belt in American Freestyle Karate, so yeah, you could say she's a real ninja, too. Get tons of free book publishing information from http://TheBookNinja.com

Chapter Fifteen

Six Great Ways a Coach Can Be Your Secret Solution to Achieving Your Goals Faster and Easier Than You Ever Thought Possible
By Leslie Cardinal

> *"Experiment to see what type of accountability and support structures will work best for you. Be open to the fact that this may change and evolve over time, too. The most important thing is to find what is best for you with your current goal."*

I'll never forget the first time I hired a coach to help me achieve some of my goals. I was working on growing my business, working on it part time as I also held down a full time corporate job. I was amazed at how helpful it was to strategize with her about my goals and to share my progress. She was genuinely pleased to hear about each step of progress. And she was a great "sounding board" so that I could talk through the challenges and obstacles I encountered. I was thrilled with my progress! Working with a coach helped me to move toward my goals faster and even more successfully than I might have otherwise.

This experience of achieving rapid success while working with a coach influenced me to become a coach myself. I loved the idea of being able to help other people in a similar way as they focused on their goals and dreams. In this chapter I want to help you as you work to achieve your goals. I'll share six great ideas I've learned from having a coach, and now from being a coach, that can help you reach your goals faster and easier. You can use these ideas and suggestions to accelerate your goal achievement and to create a great accountability structure.

A confidential thinking partner. When you have a coach, you have a person you can speak with privately about your goals. You get the benefits of their knowledge and experience, combined with yours, which is a big advantage to you. When you talk with him or her about your goals, new ideas and possibilities will often arise in the conversation, and this can help you to be even more successful in pursuing your goals.

One of the first things your coach can help you with is to more clearly and specifically define your goals and then to develop key strategies for moving forward quickly. Just having this greater level of clarity will help you immensely as you take action on your goals. You will also want to clarify the specific reasons why you want to achieve your goal. This can be a great source of inner energy to help you keep going when you encounter the normal ups and down of pursuing a goal.

A plan for regular meetings and check-ins. Another great way your coach can help you achieve success is by working with you to create an accountability structure. Experiment to find what will work best for you. Do you like to have frequent check-ins, or a little less often? Do you want to focus on your one big goal, or would you like coaching for other aspects of your life too? Do you work best with some self-imposed consequences if you don't get things done? Or are you more motivated by rewards for progress? Or a mix of both?

Set up a regular schedule of coaching sessions and accountability check-ins with your coach. You may want to enlist a trusted friend or colleague for extra support between coaching sessions. Another great accountability strategy is to keep a log or a journal of your daily actions and then share the highlights with your coach. Experiment to see what type of accountability and support structures will work best for you. Be open to the fact that this may change and evolve over time, too. The most important thing is to find what is best for you with your current goal.

A witness and a cheerleader for your progress. One of the challenges you may encounter with a big long-term goal is that it may take many months to achieve it. This long road can feel kind of lonely and it can also be a challenge to sustain your enthusiasm consistently. Look for one or two people with whom you can talk about your goals, people who will understand what you are working on and how important it is to you. Create a picture or an image of your goal that you can see regularly to remind you how much it will mean to you to achieve it.

Your coach can be a great ally in this part of the process because she really cares about your progress. In fact, your coach will be excited and delighted about your progress and your successes. He or she will understand how much effort you are putting into it, and the obstacles you have had to overcome. Just knowing that someone else is aware of your efforts can help you keep going.

Help with working through any obstacles. When you are working toward a big goal, there will be challenges and obstacles to overcome. Some of the challenges you encounter could include sustaining your own self-confidence, unexpected extra steps to reach your goal, a family emergency, a health challenge, or a delay of some type. Encountering obstacles is a normal part of the process of achieving your goals, but it can be frustrating and discouraging when they occur. So, it can be very reassuring to have people and resources that you know you can turn to when you do encounter challenges.

Your own past successes with handling obstacles can help you to have confidence that you will be able to handle future obstacles too. Use your coach as a great resource. Just talking through the situation with your coach can often help you to see the obstacle in a fresh way. She may also be able to help you identify fresh options or even ways to use the obstacle to your advantage in a creative way.

Resources to help you keep moving forward. When you are pursuing a big goal, especially a long term goal, you will often reach a point where you need extra resources. Some examples might include information, tools and equipment, encouragement, people, and fresh ideas.

Talk with your coach about this. He or she can often help you to see opportunities and resources that are already right around you. Or your coach can help you to identify people or organizations who can assist you with your challenges. She can often help you to develop creative cost-effective strategies to meet your needs and to keep moving forward.

A place to celebrate your progress. One of the best ways to sustain your energy and enthusiasm while you are working toward a big goal is to celebrate your progress. But don't wait until you have completely finished your goal. Instead, look for a way to break your goal into chunks. How will you know that you have completed each major chunk? By answering this question, you can identify key milestones and outcomes along the path to your ultimate goal.

Make a list of ways that you can celebrate each time you reach one of these milestones. This doesn't have to be expensive or elaborate. It could be as simple as treating yourself to your favorite coffee drink or celebrating with a toast at dinner with your family. Your coach can help you with breaking your goal into chunks and with ideas for celebration too. They will be genuinely delighted with your progress and eager to see you achieve every bit of progress.

These are just a few of the ways that working with your coach can help you achieve your goals. If you have never had a coach to help you with your goals, a good strategy is to work with one for an initial timeframe of 90 days. A good source for finding an experienced and well-trained coach is through the International Coach Federation at www.coachfederation.org. Tell your coach that you would like to focus on accelerating your progress, and on developing a good accountability structure, to help you move forward quickly and strongly toward your goal. Use the ideas and techniques in this chapter too, and you can be on your way to achieving new levels of success!

Leslie Ann Cardinal is a Professional Certified Coach who loves to work with entrepreneurs to make rapid progress toward their goals. She has more than 25 years of experience working with leaders and business owners in many industries. She brings her unique background of Industrial Engineering, Leadership Development, and deep knowledge of how adults learn and achieve success. Learn more by visiting www.GrowYourBusinessNow.com.

Chapter Sixteen

The Accountability Edge
By Debbie O'Grady

"What you focus on expands!"

You've had the opportunity to read the other chapters in this book and see how all the contributors have used accountability to help accomplish goals and see some of their dreams come true. These are examples of what I call *"The Accountability Edge."*

It's that edge you get by knowing what you need and want to do to succeed and then DOING those exact things. There are plenty of people out there – your competitors maybe – that know what they need to do but just aren't doing it. The people that contributed to this book understand how accountability is one of the tools that help them get things done.

I ask you this – are you reading this book because you are looking for ideas to help you build your business and make more money? Have you been working on both of these goals for a while now?

So - why is it not working for you?

I will tell you – it's probably because you are:

Not Focused,

Not Staying on Track,

And are in High Procrastination Mode!

There's a quote from Christopher Parker that fits here.

"Procrastination is like credit cards – it's a lot of fun until you get the bill"

Procrastination is that whole thing of – you get up in the morning and first thing you do is create a list of all you'll get done today. In reality, it's all the things you are *planning* to get done. Then, you get into email and there's a request to be a guest on Susie's Radio Show. Of course you need to contact Susie and the best way to catch her is on Facebook or one of the other social media platforms. You know where that leads right?

When you finally get off social media and back to your email, you see an email from someone who bought your product and can't get their login to work. Instead of contacting your VA, you decide to fix it while you are right there on the computer. Then while fixing their login, you notice your website has "the" instead of "they" in the copy. So you really quickly login to the backend of your website just to fix that one word. And yes, there's more things like this and before you know it, it's late afternoon.

You know these things needed to get done, and yes, they'll continue to need to get done, but what about the things on that list you create? You didn't get through your list of the things you planned to get done. The things that ALSO NEED to get done!

You're probably nodding and even laughing as you read this because you know this is you. You're sitting there reading this knowing you didn't finish that list of things you planned to do today. So you moved it to tomorrow's list and now you've got half of tomorrow filled with the stuff you were supposed to do today. You keep doing that day after day after day and it's frustrating. Sure, things are getting done but not as fast as you want and not always the things you really want to accomplish.

I'm going to tell you why this isn't working for you and why you're stuck here and not moving your business forward as fast as you might want. First, it's because you haven't sat down and documented your goals.

When I was a Project Manager in corporate America, I would bring my team together to lay out the schedule of tasks that needed to be accomplished in order to complete the project. Together we'd figure out what needed to be done by when and by whom and document it. This was the planning and scheduling part of the project. Once completed, everyone knew exactly what they were supposed to do and what they would be held accountable for. As the Project Manager and team leader, I went one step further. I would individually call each person into my office and ask them what were their career goals? What was it they wanted to accomplish over the next few months and years? We documented these goals and I helped them lay out a plan for how they could be accomplished. They saw how it was pretty much the same thing they had just done for the project tasks. Every week, we would get together to get status the project goals and periodically, I would call each team member in to my office and ask for status on their career goals. Again, they could see the similarities of statusing the project and their own goal accomplishments. Whenever the team reached a milestone in the project, we celebrated and whenever a team member accomplished something from their career goals list, we also celebrated that. I was teaching them about the power of accountability using accomplishments and celebrations.

Over time, most of the people from my team were promoted either within the company or got better positions within a new company. Most accomplished their career goals (some of which were to get a college degree) and I hear from some of them today telling me how they are still using those accountability techniques I taught them over 20 years ago, and how it has helped them in all aspects of their life. This is what I call "The Accountability Edge" and what I want you to get from the chapters of this book.

When I was attending one of my Mastermind meetings, my coach asked "How many of you know what your goals are off the top of your head – the ones you set six months ago?" It turned out half of the people in the room hadn't even set any goals! It was no wonder they couldn't reach them if they had not even set them. So what did our coach make us all do? She had us stop right then and there and document our next six months' goals.

AND that's the very first thing you need to do. I'm going to help you by giving you a workbook you can download so you can get your goals documented. Stop reading this chapter right now and get to your computer. Download the workbook and get your goals documented.

http://TheAccountabilityEdgeBook.com/workbook

Go ahead – do it now and then come back to reading this book.

There were 12 of us sitting in the room at that Mastermind - half of the people hadn't set goals six months earlier. But the other half in that room were really knocking it out of the park in their business. When I sat back and looked at what they were doing, I realized they were the ones who had set and documented their six month to one year goals. They knew where they were headed and they were staying on track to accomplishing exactly what they had documented.

The others were sitting there looking at each other saying "Man, we should have documented our goals!"

So what's the next thing our coach had us do? She made us tell her what our numbers were. Can you do that right now – say what all your numbers are? Are you tracking them? Do you even know what I mean when I ask about your numbers? Here are the questions you need to be asking yourself.

What are your social media numbers?

What are your revenue numbers?

How many clients do you have?

Do you know this information without going and looking it up?

Do you know how many sales conversations you need to have this month to make your revenue goal?

I run accountability programs for coaches where I am the accountability coach within their existing coaching program. I conduct the accountability calls with their clients and I've seen that the people who consistently show up for the calls and status their numbers and planned action steps – after a really short time –start to see those numbers grow and their goals accomplished. WHY? Because what you focus on expands!

Let me tell you about someone who was showing up regularly on the accountability calls I conduct for her coach. This person set and documented a revenue goal and was consistently tracking her numbers so she knew how many sales conversations she needed to have to meet that goal. Before she started tracking her numbers, what she didn't realize was that she had to be out networking to meet the people to have her sales calls with. Of course it makes sense after the fact but networking wasn't a big part of her planned action steps until she realized, by seeing and analyzing her numbers, that it was needed. Once that was known and she added networking to her action steps, she started making the number of calls per month she needed to make and started converting 3-4 new clients a month and found she was bringing in $10,000 and more of revenue a month – accomplishing her revenue goal!

You know this is what you should be doing, too. I'm not the first person to be telling you this. But are you going to finish this book and go back to doing what you've always done and getting what you've always gotten?

What I know to be true is --- we can't build a business alone. We need to be working with somebody – whether that's your actual coach, or an accountability coach, an accountability program or whatever. You need to be working with something or someone that's keeping you on track, keeping you focused and not allowing you to procrastinate. And I have to tell you, if you have an accountability partner who's a friend of yours and when you get on the phone, if they don't hold your feet to the fire, then they may be a great friend but they're a horrible accountability partner. It's not their fault. They can't help it. They are your friend.

I started out this chapter asking "Are you reading this book because you are looking for ideas to help you build your business and make more money?" You kept reading because your answer was – yes, that is exactly what you are looking for.

I told you - you aren't making money because of three things – you're not focused, you're not staying on track, and you're in high procrastination mode AND I've shown you how these are showing up in your business.

From the examples I gave, you can see how these same three things may have been showing up for some of those people I described and how they got past them. If you are sick and tired and are serious about doing something about it - you really don't have to live this way. You can get "The Accountability Edge" and see your business finally take off. The lessons you need to learn are here in this book laid out for you in every single chapter. I've made it even easier for you by capturing the tips from the different chapter authors and putting them into a list. You can download that list by going to

http://TheAccountabilityEdgeBook.com/Tips

So now you have *The Accountability Edge* that can help you accomplish your goals and be the success you strive to be. Get started today!

*Debbie O'Grady, dubbed **'Queen of Accountability'** by her clients, is a thought leader and mentor on leveraging accountability to achieve successful outcomes.*

Debbie works with forward-thinking coaches who want their clients to stay focused and on track to accomplish their goals and achieve success as rapidly as possible. The elite group of coaches that are Debbie's clients totally recognize the benefits and value of supplementing their own existing high-end coaching program with progress tracking and accountability, and know they don't want to do it themselves.

Debbie also works with individuals who understand that accountability translates to focus, progress, and success. Even if these individuals already have a coach, they recognize that Debbie's Accountability Program complements and enhances the benefits they are receiving from their current coach. The Accountability Program helps them transform the knowledge and direction imparted by their coach into action and achievement.

    Debbie@RevenueRecharge.com (email)
    www.RevenueRecharge.com (website & blog)

Made in the USA
San Bernardino, CA
13 December 2014